Lucian's
DIALOG

FIRST PUBLISHED IN 2016 BY
PDR Press
The Public Domain Review
Open Knowledge Foundation
St John's Innovation Centre
Cowley Road
Cambridge CB4 0WS
United Kingdom

pdrpress@publicdomainreview.org
www.publicdomainreview.org

EDITED AND DESIGNED BY
Nicholas Jeeves
www.nicholasjeeves.com

TYPOGRAPHY
Body text set in 9.75pt on 13pt Minion Pro Regular,
designed by Robert Slimbach, published by Adobe

ENDPAPERS
A Gathering of the Gods in the Clouds
by Cornelis van Poelenburgh, c. 1630
(Mauritshuis, The Hague)

A CIP catalogue record for this book is available
from the British Library.

10 9 8 7 6 5 4 3 2 1

Lucian's
DIALOGUES OF THE GODS

Translated from the Greek by
H. & F. FOWLER and W. TOOKE

Edited and designed by
NICHOLAS JEEVES

PRESS

CONTENTS

Such was sharpe Lucian, who reformed the Times,
Whose Gods & Temples were their Sacred Crimes.
Who gave the blinde World Eyes, & new Heavens taught,
By which the Idols from their Altars laught.
Who from dull Hypocrites plucks their Disguise,
And showd the difference between grave and wise.
Who to his Eloquence joynd all the Arts,
Admired by Rome, & Athens for his parts.
For whom noe face, or picture can be fit,
But Learning drawne in everlasting wit.

*Caption to an imagined portrait of Lucian from
the 1634 edition of Francis Hickes'* Certaine Select
Dialogues of Lucian

INTRODUCTION

LUCIAN OF SAMOSATA, who lived from c. 125 AD to c. 200 AD, was an Assyrian writer and satirist who today is perhaps best remembered for his *Vera Historia*, or *A True Story*—a fantastical tale which not only has the distinction of being one of the first science-fiction stories ever written, but is also a contender for one of the first novels.

A True Story is a stylish and brilliantly conceived work of the imagination, and readers may still delight in its descriptions of lunar life forms and interplanetary warfare, its islands of cheese and rivers of wine, and its modernistic use of celebrity cameos. But by the time of its writing Lucian was already several years into a period of literary adventurism that had brought him considerable fame— and infamy—as one of the sharpest, funniest, and most original comic writers of the Greco-Roman age. With the quartet of works consisting of *Dialogues of the Courtesans*, *Dialogues of the Dead*, *Dialogues of the Gods*, and *Dialogues of the Sea-Gods*, Lucian would not only scandalise some of the most influential and celebrated figures of the age, but in what is perhaps the best-known of these, *Dialogues of the Gods*, he would also furnish the permanent decline of belief in the gods themselves.

In *Dialogues of the Gods* Lucian conjures a series of short comic scenes in which we find the Greek gods domesticated. Here is Zeus, bluff and irritable, squabbling with Hera over his latest infidelity; there is Aphrodite, reprimanding Eros for making an old lady fall madly in love with a teenager. In *Apollo & Dionysus*, the adolescent god of wine frets about the over-endowed Priapus' "growing" interest in him; in *Pan & Hermes*, Hermes tries to duck the issue of his paternity—"how should I come by a son with horns, and with such a shaggy beard and cloven feet?"—until, that is, Pan tells him about the harem of nymphs he keeps in Arcadia. "Indeed…well—son—come hither and embrace me!"

With these twenty-six peeks behind the curtain of the great Hesiodic myths, Lucian drew up a sensational image of Heaven and the legends of its tenants, variously re-casting them as impotent, venal, greedy, needy, short-sighted, opportunistic, pathetic, sex-obsessed, and power-mad—hardly immaculate, but just like those made in their image, permanently insecure and just as prone to lowering thoughts and deeds.

These "closet dramas" would deliver a stinging blow to Greek polytheism. While philosophy was now the religion of state for urbane Athenians, the ancient beliefs were still undergoing occasional resurgences in popularity. For Lucian this was intolerable. As one of the most gifted and popular satirists of his time, and having just survived an attempt on his life by a gang of religious zealots, the gods of his forebears were ripe for his attentions.

BORN IN SAMOSATA on the banks of the Euphrates in Assyria, Lucian lived for the early part of his life under the Roman emperor Hadrian; and then as an adult under Antoninus Pius, Marcus Aurelius, and Commodus. Because there are no contemporaneous accounts of his life, not much more is known about him other than what little can be gleaned from his collected writings.

Perhaps the most revealing and charming of these is the short piece of autobiography known as *The Vision*, or *Lucian's Dream*.[1] "When my childhood was over," he writes in *The Vision*, "my father called a council to decide upon my profession." Despite Lucian expressing a keen interest in living a life of culture, his parents could not afford to finance his further education. Instead it was agreed that, having shown an aptitude for modelling small figures from the wax he had scraped from his school writing-tablets, Lucian would be apprenticed to his uncle, a sculptor.

The apprenticeship lasted one day. Lucian broke the first piece of marble he touched and was beaten with a stick in punishment—thereby giving him, as he puts it, "an introduction to art which might have been more encouraging."

From that moment on he set about acquiring the tools of culture the hard way. He spent the early part of his adulthood educating himself as he wandered in and around Ionia, Italy, and Gaul, all the while developing his skills and reputation as a rhetorician. At this he would become successful and quite

1. Reproduced in full in the appendices.

wealthy, speaking in court on behalf of paying clients, writing speeches for high-standing citizens, and publicly demonstrating his ingenuity with improvised riffs in response to suggestions called out by audiences.

He wrote extensively throughout this period—generally arch, philosophical works, composed in stylish Attic Greek, and drawing on his formidable skills as a rhetorician. Yet in his early forties he seems to have suffered what we would now call a mid-life crisis—or at least, a crisis of conscience. This may have been symptomatic of a growing suspicion that "truth", in the hands of the rhetorician, was increasingly becoming a commodity that could be bought and sold according to the interests of the highest bidder; or as Henry Fowler puts it in his introduction to *The Works of Lucian of Samosata*, "Rhetoric had been left to the legal persons whose object is not truth but victory." This idea would certainly become one of the underlying themes of Lucian's writings, and he learned to despise the self-righteous. But whatever triggered the crisis, he felt sufficiently moved to abandon the respectable life of the rhetorician and relocate permanently to Athens, where he would devote himself completely to the writing and performing of comic satires.

The journey to Athens would prove both eventful and portentous. Along the way, accompanied by his elderly parents, Lucian encountered the fraudulent priest Alexander of Abonoteichus, leader of the newly emerging cult of the snake-god Glycon. Alexander claimed that a snake in his possession was the reincarnation of the god Asclepius, and that only he, Alexander, could channel and interpret its divine prophesies. Lucian was simultaneously disgusted by the influence wielded by Alexander, and the credulity of his followers, whom he described in *Alexander the Oracle-Monger* as having "neither brains nor individuality…with only their outward shape to distinguish them from sheep."

Having identified the manifestation of the snake-god itself as nothing more than a cleverly manipulated sock puppet, Lucian was determined to expose the puppet-master. The attempt nearly cost him his life. When his turn came to ask Alexander for a prophecy, Lucian's question was as rash as it was amusing: "When will Alexander's imposture be detected?" Alexander responded with a characteristically cryptic answer, and then had Lucian followed. Discovering that Lucian was about to make a sea-crossing, Alexander paid the captain of the vessel to have Lucian and his family slain and thrown overboard. Only the captain's last-minute desire to meet his impending retirement with a clean conscience prevented the murder.[2]

Lucian would never forget the experience, and it is to be supposed that it galvanised him, honing his innate sensitivity to duplicity. With the satires that followed he began to dismantle the pillars of hypocrisy wherever he saw them. With *Dialogues of the Courtesans*, he sketched a merciless portrait of the hetaerae — the high-status prostitutes of Athens — and their puffed-up clients. He built on these with *Dialogues of the Dead*, in which he ridiculed the vain expectations of a host of recently departed celebrities arriving in the afterlife, including the eminent philosophers Diogenes and Polystratus, the warrior Hannibal, and Kings Philip and Alexander of Macedon. Having dealt with the rich, the famous, and the mighty, he turned his gaze upwards, to the very peaks of Mount Olympus. With *Dialogues of the Gods* and *of the Sea-Gods*, he would visit his wits on Heaven, and taunt the gods themselves.

The fictions he produced thereafter would become among the finest examples of satire that we have. Here we might pause for a moment to consider what the world of satirical comedy, from *Don Quixote* to *The Office*, might owe him. Certainly as much as is owed to Aristophanes, and perhaps much more than that.

WHILE LUCIAN IS treasured by classicists, today his extensive achievements seem hardly to rank at all in the wider public consciousness. In contrast with his venerable forebears, he has slipped into relative obscurity.

It was not always like that. From the middle Renaissance into the late 1800s Lucian was among the most widely-read of the "Greeks" in Europe, largely thanks to the efforts of the great Dutch theologian Erasmus and his English friend Thomas More. Sharing an appreciation for Lucian's amusing scepticism and the elegance of his prose style, together they produced, in the early 1500s,

---

2. The full story of Lucian's encounter with Alexander is recounted in *Alexander the Oracle-Monger*, written ten years after the high priest's death. It remains the only known first-hand account of the snake cult, and its enigmatic but decidedly phoney leader.

the first major translation of his works into Latin. The project, which took several years to complete, would become a publishing sensation, going through more than thirty editions in Erasmus' and More's lifetimes alone.[3]

Not everyone was pleased to see it. Thanks to the international appeal of the Erasmus-More translations, by 1590 Lucian's entire canon had been placed on the *Index Librorum Prohibitorum*, the Vatican's catalogue of texts considered to be heretical, anti-clerical, or obscene, and thus too hot for public consumption. The arrival of the Protestant Reformation hadn't done Lucian much good either: Luther despised him for his mocking of religious—and in one or two instances, specifically Christian—values and practices.[4]

Yet despite such prejudices Lucian's popularity continued to grow rapidly—not least of all in England, where his dialogues found their way onto school curricula. Thomas Linacre, Thomas More's old teacher, believed that "Your toil will become light and amusing and your progress sure, if you will only read a little Lucian every day." And so it proved, as Lucian was endorsed by a new generation of schoolmasters, each in agreement that his sharp wit, broad humour, and matchless style provided the perfect means by which a young lad might be encouraged to attend to his Latin.

A number of English translations soon followed. First was Francis Hickes' *Certaine Select Dialogues of Lucian* of 1634, updated and republished in 1664 to include Jasper Mayne's *Part of Lucian made English from the Originall*. Ferrand Spence's more extensive *Lucian's Works* of 1684 was the first to make use of vernacular English, a decision which infuriated the esteemed poet and translator John Dryden. In his essay "The Life of Lucian", which would preface the four-volume *Works of Lucian* of 1711, Dryden remarked of Lucian that "No Man is so great a Master of Irony, as our Author"—but of Spence, thought it "not worth my while to rake into the filth of so scandalous a Version...he makes

---

3. The influence of the project on the works and futures of both men cannot be overstated: Erasmus' *In Praise of Folly* of 1509, which would go on to play such a key role in the birth of the Reformation, was indisputably "Lucianic"; More's 1516 novel *Utopia* owed much to themes and ideas drawn from *A True Story*.

4. Lucian thus providing an enjoyably ironic point of consensus between the two factions, a situation that would surely have delighted the old rogue.

[Lucian] speak in the Stile and Language of a Jack-Pudding, not a Master of Eloquence...for the fine Raillery, and Attique Salt of Lucian, we find the gross Expressions of Billings-Gate, or More-Fields and Bartholomew Fair." [5]

For the next sixty years or so, "Dryden's Lucian", as it became known, [6] would serve as the standard. Yet as Lucian became ever more popular, and as the demand for new editions grew, so the translations kept coming—and with them a series of alternating editorial visions. John Carr's *Dialogues of Lucian* of 1773 succeeded in being vivid, earthy, and companionable, directed as it was towards the general reader rather than the classical scholar. Thomas Francklin's *Works of Lucian* of 1780 took a more academic approach, a rebuke to Carr that resulted in a more respectable, but considerably less fun, translation. William Tooke's *Lucian of Samosata* of 1820 might be thought of as a "Goldilocks" edition—pitched just right, with Tooke allowing Lucian's schoolboy humour, his sly philosophy, and his smart prose to shine through just as he found it in the Greek, untroubled by any notions of incongruity.

Yet as the eighteenth century drew to a close, Lucian slowly began to fall out of favour. Victorian attitudes to propriety prevailed, and schoolboys had their Lucian substituted with Ovid, Horace, and Virgil. The story might have ended there, had relief not come from the unlikeliest of places—a small tomato plantation on the island of Guernsey. From here, two classically educated brothers had noticed that one of their heroes needed rescuing from obscurity, and meant to do something about it.

IT IS SIMPLISTIC to say that the Fowlers' translation, published in 1905, would prove itself to be the finest yet. It is more likely that, being in the most modern form of English, it is the most immediately appealing to today's reader. Yet it is

---

5. Fair enough. In 2008, Black Box published an edition of *Dialogues of the Gods* in which Zeus accuses Eros of "kissing my ass", and Poseidon wonders if his brother has caught "some sort of STD". In light of such things it becomes easier to appreciate Dryden's rebuke.

6. Thanks to this appellation, the 1711 translation is sometimes erroneously attributed to Dryden in its entirety. Dryden had a hand in the editing and wrote its famous introduction, but in fact the book is the work of "several eminent hands" including Walter Moyle, Sir Henry Shere, and Charles Mount.

fulsome in its appreciation of the spectrum of Lucian's capabilities, and positively sparkles with a kind of school-boyish enthusiasm that has the virtue of being the product of exactly that.

Born in 1858, Henry Fowler was educated first at Rugby, and then at Balliol College, Oxford. After leaving Balliol with a second-class degree he secured a position as a schoolmaster. It was not to be a happy career choice. Though he was teaching Latin and Greek—subjects which he had loved, and at which he had excelled, since he was a schoolboy—he was not really cut out for the job. After seventeen years and an unfortunate series of misunderstandings over a promotion, aged 41 he resigned his post and set out for London to make his way as a writer.

Meanwhile his brother Frank, twelve years his junior, had been studying at Peterhouse, Cambridge. Frank's academic career had followed in similar style to Henry's, with a promising start ultimately leading to a third-class degree and much disappointment. From time-to-time Henry would visit Frank at Cambridge where they would share their passion for the Greek and Roman classics, and discuss their ambitions to collaborate on something as soon as they could manage it.

Henry's first year as a writer proved to be not much more fruitful than his life as a teacher. He wrote a few essays and articles for titles including *Punch*, *The Anglo-Saxon Review*, and *The Spectator*, but enjoyed only modest success. By the spring of 1903, at the age of 42, Henry found himself at a low ebb. Behind him lay an ungratifying and only moderately successful career as a schoolmaster and journalist; ahead, a number of possible paths, the most tempting of these now being an invitation to grow tomatoes with his younger brother Frank in Guernsey where, in their spare time, they might finally act on their plans to write together. Henry chose to accept Frank's offer and shortly afterwards, in-between their labours among the tomato plants, they began working on their first project, a new translation of the works of Lucian.

There were a number of good reasons for choosing Lucian. First, the most recent translation, a selected works by the Cambridge scholar Howard Williams in 1888, was considered to be unsatisfactory by the Fowlers. Second, they felt that the great satirist had been neglected for too many years, having slowly fallen out of fashion, and that a mass-market revival was due. Third, Oxford University had recently begun publishing a series of translations of Greek and Roman classics under the Clarendon Press imprint, and Henry felt that a complete Lucian would make an ideal addition to the catalogue.

But there was also another, more carefully concealed reason: Henry saw some interesting parallels between his own lack of religious faith and Lucian's questioning of the religious authorities of his day. Henry had little time for religion and the "airs of intellectual superiority" he felt it engendered. As Jenny McMorris quotes in her excellent biography of Henry, *The Warden of English* (OUP, 2001), "Thirty years ago I thought religious belief true; twenty years ago doubtful; ten years ago false; and now it is (for me, of course) merely absurd." It is doubtful that Henry shared any of this with his publishers. He was canny enough to sense that it would not only prove an unhelpful confidence, but that there were enough good reasons to persuade Oxford to fund the book's publication anyway without invoking dangerous personal ones.

The commission to translate Lucian agreed, Henry and Frank divided the Lucian workload between them. The pieces which Henry translated are marked in the books with an "H"; Frank's with an "F". Those translations they found more challenging, and on which they thus found it necessary to collaborate, were marked "H. F." By this method they were, by the close of 1904, able to present to Oxford their complete works of Lucian.

Well—not the *complete* works. During their initial proposal to Oxford, Henry had noted that several of the *Dialogues* might need to be expunged so as not to offend the decency of their readership (who were not, after all, only scholars or students, but also more general readers). Not wishing to pre-empt which pieces would be acceptable to Oxford and which not, the job of censor was willingly handed over to the university Vice-Chancellor William Walter Merry. On this occasion at least Merry was quite liberal with his blue pencil. In *Dialogues of the Gods* alone he excised seven of the twenty-six.[7]

The six dialogues which would have most obviously made Oxford nervous

---

7. Though curiously, he only excised three of the ribald *Dialogues of the Courtesans*, a decision which today is hard to fathom considering some of his other rulings.

were these: *Zeus & Ganymede*, and the sequel *Hera & Zeus*, which together detail Zeus' sexual obsession with, and abduction of, the boy Ganymede; *Hermes & Helios*, which references the conception of Heracles over three long nights of athletic lovemaking; *Apollo & Hermes*, in which Hermes relates the story of Hephaestus catching Aphrodite and Ares in bed together; *Pan & Hermes*, in which the goat-like Pan claims Hermes as his father, and details how this might have come about; and *Apollo & Dionysus*, which contains explicit references to the well-hung and permanently erect Priapus.

As to why the seventh, *Poseidon & Hermes*, was excised is a bit of a mystery. The dialogue deals with the birth of Dionysus from Zeus' leg. There is nothing in it that is particularly shocking even to delicate sensibilities, and the story of how Dionysus was born would already have been known to anyone with even a casual familiarity with the Greek myths. Perhaps it was the idea that a man might give birth on behalf of a woman that bothered Merry; perhaps it was the passing references to adultery and hermaphroditism—though one imagines that these could easily have been removed without damaging the text too severely. Whatever his reasons, it seems we will never know exactly what he saw in it that so exercised his blue pencil.

Given that the edition of *Dialogues of the Gods* that you now hold in your hands re-unites the *Dialogues* (filling in the gaps with tweaked versions of the Tooke translation), the remaining expurgated items deserve some particular attention, for they are among the most interesting of the set—though this is quite possibly *because* of their wickedness (which is rather a lowering thought in itself, but there we have it.)

Of the seven excised dialogues, *Zeus & Ganymede* and *Hera & Zeus* would have been the most obviously problematic. In the first of these, Lucian sets the familiar mythological scene in which Zeus takes on the appearance of an eagle so that he may swoop down on the comely shepherd-boy Ganymede and carry him up to heaven forever. "Kiss me, you fine little fellow!" says Zeus on their arrival. "You are now an inmate of Heaven. Instead of milk and cheese you will eat ambrosia and drink nectar." Ganymede is understandably distraught. "But where am I to sleep at night?" he asks innocently—to which Zeus replies, "Little numbskull, I brought you away that you may sleep with me!"

In *Hera and Zeus*, Zeus tries to justify the presence of his new *erômenos* to his furious wife. She is having none of it. "Zeus! I hope never to proceed so far in condescension as to let my lips be contaminated by a Phrygian shepherd-boy—and such an effeminate stripling too!" To which Zeus replies, "Mind your language, madam—this effeminate stripling, this Phrygian shepherd-boy, this delicate youth…Ah, goodness, I had best say no more, lest I overheat myself!"

The remaining four dialogues on the blacklist are not nearly so contentious, and with them we find we can return, with some relief, to the lighter side of Lucian's palette. *Hermes & Helios* is a bit of racy tittle-tattle in which Zeus sends orders to Helios, the sun-god, to stay in for a few days so that Zeus can spend an unnaturally long night copulating with Alcmene. Merry would only have seen fit to censor it due to its bawdiness, a highlight of which is when Helios chunters about how, in his day, "such things did not use to happen…Whereas now, for the sake of one graceless woman…poor mankind must live miserably in darkness all the while, and—thanks to the amorous temperament of the king of the gods!—there they must sit waiting in that long obscurity, till this great athlete you speak of is finished!"

Apollo & Hermes is similarly risqué. Here Hermes relates to his companion the story of how Hephaestus has managed, at last, to catch his wife Aphrodite in bed with Ares, the god of war. Trapping them in a magical net like a pair of eels, Hephaestus calls everyone together to witness the adultery for themselves. Despite this highly embarrassing situation Hermes confides that, even so, "I could not help thinking that Ares, when I beheld him so entangled with the fairest of all the goddesses, was in a very enviable situation."

In *Pan & Hermes*, Pan claims Hermes as his father. Not only is Pan boastful of his many sexual conquests, but there is an uncomfortable moment in which we are impelled to figure out just how goat-like Hermes was when he made love to Penelope—a touch of bestiality that did not go unnoticed by Merry.

Finally, *Apollo & Dionysus*, in which Dionysus first brings up the subject of Aphrodite's variously-natured children as a preamble to an embarrassing tale in which he is cornered by Priapus and his giant penis. He is clearly worried about this encounter and what it means but, like a schoolboy wanting to ask a friendly uncle about girls, tries to approach the subject from another angle so as to make his enquiry seem rather more casual, and therefore less excruciating. Regarding Merry's blue pencil, this one rather speaks for itself.

In 1905, the four-volume set *The Works of Lucian of Samosata* was published to great critical acclaim, and remained in print until 1939. Today the OUP have only the dual-language Loeb Library editions and C. D. N. Costa's slim volume of *Selected Dialogues* in their catalogue. In the intervening years the Fowler text has entered the public domain and is occasionally re-printed by smaller publishers, to varying standards. It is nonetheless pleasing to know that, for anyone still wishing to discover Lucian, it is in the lively company of Henry and Frank that they will most likely find themselves, even over a hundred years later.

The Fowlers capitalised on their successful partnership the following year with their first best-seller, a book of English usage and grammar they called *The King's English*. Frank died in 1918 aged 47 from tuberculosis. He was much missed by Henry, who dedicated his next book, *Modern English Usage*, to Frank, writing, "he had a nimbler wit, a better sense of proportion, and a more open mind, than his twelve-year-older partner." Henry died in 1933 aged 75, and would be remembered by *The Times* as "a lexicographical genius" thanks to his work on these and, more notably, the first *Concise Oxford English Dictionary*.

As for Lucian himself, the details surrounding his death remain something of a mystery. The story that he was torn to pieces by dogs is a well-known myth propagated in the tenth century by the compiler of the encyclopedic Suda, a Christian who was unimpressed with Lucian's perceived mockery of the faith. Lucian was largely, but not entirely, innocent of the accusation: his *Death of Peregrinus* had made characteristic fun of the newly emerging religion, and it remains one of the few first-hand accounts of its earliest expressions. He saw out his days in Egypt, having been pastured by the emperor Commodus into an easy and well-paid legal post. We know that he performed his dialogues there, and that he suffered badly from gout, an affliction about which—naturally—he wrote a play, featuring the goddess Gout herself. As Fowler writes in his introduction to *The Works of Lucian of Samosata*, "whether the goddess was appeased by it, or carried him off, we cannot tell."

APOLOGY

When I first set about assembling this new edition of the complete *Dialogues of the Gods*, and having decided to use the Fowlers' translation as the basis for this, the first problem to resolve was the issue of the seven excised dialogues.

To remedy this I have turned to the Tooke translation of 1820. It is, for all its 85-year age difference, much closer in style and in spirit to the Fowler translation than the more youthful, but comparatively much less fun, Williams translation of 1888. From here I have occasionally and very carefully edited certain words or phrases in both translations, particularly those which may otherwise have leapt out as being archaic or unhelpfully idiomatic. The resulting text has, I hope, an evenness of tone such that the reader will not spot the seams. Such a process can never be a perfect science but I hope that readers will make this small allowance, if only to be able to enjoy the dialogues more consistently and completely. For a quick guide to who translated which dialogue, the contents page contains the relevant initials aligned to each.

There are, however, some more substantial differences between this edition and its predecessors, principally in the decision to depart from the traditional ordering of the dialogues so as to make the whole more narratively consistent. (There is, as discussed in the appendices, some precedent for this, so I don't feel I am taking too great a liberty.) This is a consideration to the modern reader as I felt it was jarring, for example, to have Zeus call on Hermes for assistance several dialogues before Hermes is born; or to have Dionysus mentioned in passing when he is yet to emerge from Zeus' leg. There are many such inconsistencies throughout the dialogues in their original ordering; some still remain, though there are now fewer of them.

It is doubtful that any of this would have mattered to Lucian or his audiences. The *Dialogues* were not produced as a book in the way we would think of such a thing today; it is more likely that Lucian would have considered each of the dialogues as discrete vignettes, albeit existing within a larger literary scheme.

A further addition to this volume is the preceding list of *Dramatis Dei*. With these mini-biographies of the gods, readers new or recently returned to the Greek myths will be able, if they so wish, to familiarise themselves with some of the key relationships and bits of pertinent background for each of the characters appearing in the *Dialogues*. Lucian would never have had to do this, of course, as the gods and their mythical histories would have been as familiar to his first audiences as our twenty-first-century celebrities are to us.

In the same spirit I have also added short introductions to each dialogue. Other editions have done similarly to a greater or lesser extent and, when reading through these, I always found this occasional narrative voice helpful, carrying the reader between one dramatic scene and the next.

The final change is one that takes us the furthest from convention: the setting-out of the texts themselves. Unlike a novel—the form of which supports the use of "he said", or "said so-and-so" to prevent the reader from getting lost in the dialogue—in a playbook every bit of dialogue is conventionally preceded by the speaker's name, like this:

Hephaestus. What are your orders, Zeus? You sent for me, and here I am, with such an edge to my axe as would cleave a stone at one blow.

Zeus. That's right. Just split my head in half, will you?

Hephaestus. You think I am mad, perhaps? Seriously, now, what can I do for you?

Zeus. What I say: crack my skull. Any insubordination, now, and you shall taste my resentment; and it will not be the first time.

This is how Lucian arranged the dialogues in manuscript, and how they were laid out, more or less, by subsequent scholars and publishers.[1] From the reader's point of view it is at least logical: it separates the two voices and we now know who is talking and when. But as a reading experience this arrangement can also be distracting, the flow of the dialogue interrupted by the repeated insertion of each speaker's name.

1. See Appendix (i) for further examples and variants of these.

APO Quere' Neptunum, cui modo Tridē-
tem furatus est. Quære' etiam Martem,
nam et huius gladium e uagina clandesti-
nus extraxit. De' me ipso nihil plane' di-
cam, quem arcu et sagittis exarmauit.
VVL Hæc, qui recens ortus et uix infasci-
is mouebatur? APO Probe' scies Vulcane,
si paululum ad te' accesserit VVL Atqui
iam accessit. APO Ecquid igitur, sunt ne'
tibi omnia instrumenta, ita ut nullum e-
orum amiseris? VVL Omnia sane' o A-
pollo APO Tamen aduerte' quæso exacti.
VVL Per Iouem forcipem non uideo APO
Eum uspiam in fasciis pueri conspicies VVL
Adeon aduncis est manibus, ut in materno

c 2

Page from a mid-16th-century manuscript in Latin containing ten of the *Dialogues of the Gods* translated by Livio Guidolotto, apostolic assistant to Pope Leo X. Note the rubricated names of the gods (VVL for Vulcan / Hephaestus, APO for Apollo) separating each speaker's parts within a continuous text. Source: Biblioteca comunale degli Intronati, Siena.

The thinking behind the design of this edition of *Dialogues of the Gods* was to see if we could, with some careful re-thinking of convention, do away with the names; to create a system of text-setting that would allow us to enjoy the dialogues as easily as if they were scenes from a novel, or a film—instinctively, in the moment, without having to consciously think all the time about who is doing the speaking.

The design system I have thus imposed on the book was largely inspired by ideas of stages, rather than pages—as when we see a stand-up comedian, for example, relating to us a conversation between two people: within the confines of the stage, he stands over *here* when doing *this* person, over *there* when doing *that* person. By assigning a separate physical space to each voice, the performer ensures that we never lose track of who is speaking—and so it is, I hope, with the arrangement of the voices in this book.

DRAMATIS DEI

ZEUS. Son of the Titans Cronos and Rhea; now king of the gods, ruling the earth with his aegis and thunderbolts, and a very short temper. A slave to his desires, he often recruits other gods to assist him in his latest lusty scheme.

HERA. Wife of Zeus and, as is so often the case among the mythical beings of ancient Greece, his sister. Traditionally caricatured as a jealous nag—though we might sympathise considering what she has to contend with. Also the mother of Hephaestus.

HEPHAESTUS. Olympian blacksmith and son of Hera. A cripple as a result of Zeus' fury, he is often mocked for being sooty and sweaty as a result of his labours at the forge. He is routinely engaged as a sort of Olympian odd-job man. Endures a rather challenging marriage to Aphrodite.

APHRODITE. For a goddess of love, Aphrodite's own love life is painfully complicated, with husband Hephaestus possibly her half-brother; and lover Ares, the god of war, also probably a brother. This is not to mention affairs with Hermes, Poseidon, and Dionysus (all close relatives). Perhaps unsurprisingly, she has three of the most exotic children in Heaven: Eros, the god of love; Hermaphroditus, of both and neither sex; and the over-endowed Priapus, who exists in a permanent state of arousal.

ARES. Son of Zeus and Hera, Ares is the god of war, and lover of Aphrodite (to Hephaestus' great frustration). Of a martial nature, with all the dangerous aspirations that go with it.

EROS. Son of Aphrodite, and god of love. He uses his magical bow and arrows to entangle in love whomever he pleases. Though ancient, he bears the form of a child, an image he exploits when he is inevitably censured by his love-struck targets. His best customer is, naturally, Zeus.

HERMES. The exceptionally gifted result of Zeus' affair with Maia, daughter of the Titan Atlas. Hermes seemingly has it all—looks, wisdom, speed, cunning, charisma, and charm. As a result he is routinely called upon by any god needing expert assistance.

PAN. Goaty god of nature and sexuality; associate of Dionysus, "companion" to the nymphs, governor of Arcadia and—he asserts—son of Hermes.

DIONYSUS. God of wine and revelry, leading by example. Another of Zeus' sons, this time by the mortal Semele. The means by which he is born is typically irregular—from a gash in Zeus' leg—but he goes on to make a great name for himself. Severely disapproved of by Hera.

LETO. Another of Zeus' lovers, and mother of Apollo and Artemis. Despised by Hera, who perceives this new generation as a challenge to the birthright of her own son, the unfortunate Hephaestus.

APOLLO. God of music, poetry and prophecy; and son of Zeus by the Titan-born beauty Leto. Famous for communicating through the Oracle at Delphi, and talented with a bow (just like his sister, Artemis). Traditionally portrayed as one of the most intelligent and complex gods in Greek mythology—though he is curiously luckless for one supposedly so in tune with destiny.

ARTEMIS. Sister of Apollo; goddess of the hunt, and an untameable, die-hard independent. She appears to have very little time either for the goings-on in Heaven, or indeed for men—much to the frustration of Eros.

ATHENA. Goddess of wisdom and war, and Zeus' daughter by Metis (his first wife). Born from Zeus' head in full battle-armour, she, like Artemis, cherishes her independence.

GANYMEDE. A mortal boy, a shepherd, and very beautiful. Zeus develops a passion to possess him completely—once again, much to Hera's horror.

HELIOS. A Titan and god of the sun, Helios rides out on his solar chariot every morning to deliver the day. His son, Phaeton, is the cause of much trouble when he convinces his father to let him take the reins.

SELENE. Goddess of the moon, and sister of the sun-god Helios. Here she fixes her passions on the perpetually-sleeping hunter Endymion (why he sleeps is another story). She will, despite her despair over this typically mythical situation, eventually bear him fifty children.

POSEIDON. Zeus' brother, in charge of the sea. Plays a small role in the *Dialogues*; his part is naturally extended in the sequel, *Dialogues of the Sea-Gods*.

PROMETHEUS. A Titan who has a bit of history with Zeus. He sided with Zeus during the war against the Titans, but soon after began to irritate him on a cosmic scale: inventing humans, stealing for them the secret of fire, and diddling Zeus out of his sacrificial dinners. His punishment: lashed to a rock for an eternity while vultures peck daily at his liver.

HERACLES. More popularly known by his Roman name, Hercules. The son of Zeus by the mortal Alcmene and perhaps the most famous of the Greek heroes. Books are devoted to his origins and doings, which include causing Hera's bosom to squirt out the Milky Way; strangling snakes as a baby; killing his wife and child in a fit of divine madness; and a long round of lion-slaying, horse-stealing and hydra-decapitating.

ASCLEPIUS. God of medicine and healing, and son of Apollo by the mortal Coronis. Lived a mortal life on earth as a supernaturally talented healer thanks to a snake licking his ear. He became so effective in his ministrations that people stopped dying. He was thus slain by Zeus and brought to Heaven so that natural order might be restored.

IAPETUS. Iapetus himself does not make an appearance in the *Dialogues*, but he is mentioned quite prominently on occasion in the context of his great age. He is one of the original Titans, who ruled the world in the aeons before Zeus came to power.

CASTOR & POLLUX. Twins who are only mentioned in the *Dialogues,* but who remain an important part of Greek mythology. A complicated pair—they share a mother, Leda, but each has a different father: Castor is the son of the mortal Tyndareus; Pollux the son of Zeus. Better known today by their place in the night sky; they would be transformed into the constellation Gemini.

DIALOGUES OF THE GODS

1   "Come on, a good lusty stroke, and quick about it."

Panicking in response to a dire prophesy, ZEUS *has eaten the pregnant Metis whole, hoping to avoid the birth of the warrior goddess Athena— who, it is said, will one day usurp him. Unfortunately for Zeus, the foetus has taken up residence in his head, and is almost due, giving him a splitting headache. Desperate to relieve the pain, he asks* HEPHAESTUS, *the blacksmith, to turn his hand to a bit of Olympian-style midwifery…*

HEPHAESTUS   &
                ZEUS

What are your orders, Zeus? You sent for me, and
here I am, with such an edge to my axe as would
cleave a stone at one blow.

> That's right, Hephaestus. Just split my head in half,
> will you?

You think I am mad, perhaps? Seriously, now, what
can I do for you?

> What I say: crack my skull. Any insubordination,
> now, and you shall taste my resentment; and it will
> not be the first time. Come on, a good lusty stroke,
> and quick about it. I am in the pangs of travail; my
> brain is in a whirl.

Mind you, the consequences may be serious: the axe
is sharp, and will prove but a rough midwife.

> Hew away, and fear nothing. I know what I am about.

H'm. I don't like it: however, one must obey orders…
Why, what have we here? A maiden in full armour!
This is no joke, Zeus. You might well be waspish,
with this great girl growing up beneath your pia
mater; in armour, too! You have been carrying a regular barracks on your shoulders all this time. And so
active! See, she is dancing a war-dance, with shield

and spear in full swing. She is like one inspired; and
(what is more to the point) she is extremely pretty,
and has come to marriageable years in these few
minutes; those grey eyes, even, look well beneath a
helmet. Zeus, I claim her as the fee for my midwifery.

Impossible! She is determined to remain a maid for
ever. Not that I have any objection, personally.

That is all I want. You can leave the rest to me. I'll
carry her off this moment.

Well, if you think it so easy. But I am sure it is a hope-
less case.

2 "I offer you information which is invaluable…"

PROMETHEUS, *in punishment for his sins—inventing men and women, stealing the secret of fire from Olympus, swindling ZEUS out of the tastiest bits of sacrificial offerings—is chained to a distant rock, and attacked every day by a vulture who feasts on his liver. But he retains his valuable talent for prophecy. Presently, Zeus is on his way to see Thetis, the latest object of his affections—but does Prometheus have information for him that might buy back his freedom?*

PROMETHEUS   &
                ZEUS

Release me, Zeus; I have suffered enough.

> Release you? You? Why, by rights your irons should
> be heavier, you should have the whole weight of
> Caucasus upon you, and instead of one, a dozen
> vultures, not just pecking at your liver, but scratching
> out your eyes. You made these abominable human
> creatures to vex us, you stole our fire, you invented
> women. I need not remind you how you overreached
> me about the meat-offerings; my portion, bones
> disguised in fat: yours, all the good.

And have I not been punished enough—riveted to
the Caucasus all these years, feeding your bird (on
which all worst curses light!) with my liver?

> 'Tis not a fraction of your deserts.

Consider, I do not ask you to release me for nothing.
I offer you information which is invaluable.

> Promethean wiles!

Wiles? To what end? You can find the Caucasus
another time; and there are chains to be had, if you
catch me cheating.

> Tell me first the nature of your 'invaluable' offer.

If I tell you your present errand correctly, will that
convince you that I can prophesy too?

>It will.

You are bound on a little visit to Thetis…

>Right so far. And the rest?

Have no dealings with her. As sure as she conceives
by you, your child shall deal you the hand you dealt
to your own—

>I shall lose my kingdom, you would say?

Avert it, Fate! I say only that intercourse portends
this issue.

>Well, then—Thetis, farewell! And for this, Pro-
>metheus, Hephaestus shall set you free.

3

"I like being in love, only I don't like all this fuss."

As is becoming clear, ZEUS likes being in love—and often. Over the years, in order to improve his chances, he has sought the help of the eternal child EROS, the god of love. Eros' standard strategy is to have Zeus visit earth as a bull, or a swan, or an eagle—something magical and appealing. But after the Thetis affair and a near-miss with destiny, Zeus begins to suspect that Eros is making a ninny of him, and pays him a visit with some heavy-looking chains…

EROS   &
                        ZEUS

You might let me off, Zeus! I suppose it was rather
naughty of me; but there!—I am but a child; a
wayward child.

> A child, and born before Iapetus was even thought
> of? You bad old man! Just because you have no beard,
> and no white hairs, are you going to pass yourself off
> for a child?

And what great harm has this old man ever done
you, that you should talk of chains?

> Ask your own guilty conscience, what harm. The
> pranks you have played on me! Satyr, bull, swan,
> eagle, shower of gold—I have been everything in my
> time, and I have you to thank for it. You never by any
> chance make the women fall in love with *me*; no one
> is ever smitten with *my* charms, that I have noticed.
> No, there must be magic in it always; I must be kept
> well out of sight. They like the bull or the swan well
> enough: but once let them set eyes on me, and they
> are frightened out of their lives.

Well, of course. They are but mortals; the sight of
Zeus is too much for them.

> Then why are Branchus and Hyacinth so fond of
> Apollo?

Daphne ran away from him in the end, remember, in
spite of his beautiful hair and his smooth chin. Now,
shall I tell you the way to win hearts? Keep that aegis
of yours quiet, and leave the thunderbolt at home;
make yourself as smart as you can; curl your hair and
tie it up with a bit of ribbon, get a purple cloak, and
gold-bespangled shoes, and march forth to the music
of flute and drum—and see if you don't get a finer
following than Dionysus, for all his Maenads.

                Pooh! I'll win no hearts on such terms.

Oh, in that case, don't fall in love. Nothing could be
simpler.

                I dare say; but I like being in love, only I don't like
all this fuss. Now mind—if I let you off, it is on this
understanding.

4

"One would swear he had practised
petty larceny in the womb."

*There's a new baby in Heaven—Hermes, Zeus' son by Maia, one of the
seven daughters of Atlas. He is destined to have one of the most impressive,
and lengthy, CVs in Olympus. Though still a babe-in-arms, already he is
demonstrating his prodigious talent for fleetness of foot—and lightness
of finger, as HEPHAESTUS and APOLLO are finding out...*

HEPHAESTUS &
APOLLO

Have you seen Maia's baby, Apollo? Such a pretty
little thing, with a smile for everybody; you can see it
is going to be a treasure.

> That baby a treasure? Well, in mischief, Iapetus is
> young beside it.

Why, what harm can it do, only just born?

> Ask Poseidon; it stole his trident. Ask Ares; he was
> surprised to find his sword gone out of the scabbard.
> Not to mention myself, disarmed of bow and arrows.

Never! That infant? He has hardly found his legs yet;
he is not even out of his baby-linen.

> Ah, you will find out, Hephaestus, if he gets within
> reach of you.

He has been.

> Well? All your tools safe? None missing?

Of course not.

> I advise you to make sure.

Zeus! Where are my tongs?

Ah, you will find them among the baby-linen.

So light-fingered! One would swear he had practised
petty larceny in the womb.

> And you don't know what a glib young chatterbox he
> is; and, if he has his way, he is to be our errand-boy!
> Yesterday he challenged Eros—tripped up his heels
> somehow, and had him on his back in a twinkling;
> before the applause was over, he had taken the
> opportunity of a congratulatory hug from Aphrodite
> to steal her girdle; Zeus had not done laughing before
> his sceptre was gone. If the thunderbolt had not been
> too heavy, and very hot, he would have made away
> with that too.

The child has some spirit in him, by your account.

> Spirit, yes—and some music, moreover, young as
> he is.

How can you tell that?

> He picked up a dead tortoise somewhere or other,
> and contrived an instrument with it. He fitted horns
> to it, with a cross-bar, stuck in pegs, inserted a bridge,
> and played a sweet tuneful thing that made an old
> harper like me quite envious. Even at night, Maia
> was saying, he does not stay in Heaven; he goes down
> poking his nose into Hades—on a thieves' errand, no
> doubt. Then he has a pair of wings, and he has made
> himself a magic wand, which he uses for marshalling
> souls—convoying the dead to their place.

HEPHAESTUS   &
                    APOLLO

Ah, I gave him that, for a toy.

              And by way of payment he stole your tongs.

Well remembered; I must go and get them; you may
be right about the baby-linen…

5

"In consequence of a hard labour,
he finds himself rather weak..."

The sea-god POSEIDON *pays a call on his brother Zeus. But* HERMES
*has some news for his uncle Poseidon: Zeus is pregnant again—this time
not in the head, but in the leg—and is not at home to visitors...*

POSEIDON   &
                  HERMES

Is Zeus free to be spoken to, Hermes?

        Not at the moment, Poseidon.

Come, come—announce me, at least.

        I ask you not to be troublesome, uncle; I tell you that
        at present he has no time, and that you cannot be
        allowed to see him.

He is perhaps shut away with Hera?

        No; quite another matter.

A-ha, I understand! Somebody else?

        No, not that either: in short he is… not well.

How can that be, Hermes? It is incomprehensible.

        It is so much, that I am ashamed to speak of it.

Surely you may speak of it to your uncle?

        Well—he is just now delivered of a son.

Are you mad! He delivered, you say? Who then is the
father? Has he been an hermaphrodite all this while,

without our knowing? By any swelling in his belly
at least, no symptoms of his pregnancy were visible.

> That's true; but the child lays not where it commonly
> does.

It therefore came from his head, as Athena did? I say,
his head is an excellent breeder!

> Not so this time. He was big (since it must out) in the
> thick of the thigh with a child of Semele's.

Nature has been very liberal with him, it must be
said. But who is this Semele?

> A Thebaness, the daughter of Cadmus, who was with
> child by him—

And now he has given birth on her behalf?

> I see that the affair seems ridiculous to you; I will
> tell you how it happened. Hera, to whose jealousy
> you are no stranger, artfully came over poor, simple
> Semele, and persuaded her to request of Zeus that he
> would visit her in all his glory—with all the lightning
> and thunder. Zeus granted her request: but the house
> was set on fire by it, and Semele herself was struck
> with lightning. As he could not save the mother, he
> ordered me at least to cut the child out of her and
> bring it to him. She being only seven months gone,
> and therefore the embryo not full-timed, he made an
> opening in his thigh, and stuck it in until it was ripe
> for birth. And now at the end of nine months he has

                    brought the child into the world; but in consequence
                    of a hard labour he finds himself rather weak.

And where is the child now?

                    I am ordered to convey him to Nyssa, there to be
                    brought up by the nymphs under the name Dionysus.

So, my illustrious brother is therefore at the same
time father and mother of little Dionysus.

                    So it seems. But I can dally here no longer. I must run
                    and fetch water for him, and provide the necessary
                    for a person newly brought to bed.

6

"We have come to our journey's end.
Kiss me, you fine little fellow!"

ZEUS *has fixed his passions on* GANYMEDE, *an innocent shepherd boy of outstanding beauty. So smitten is Zeus with the lad's charms that he means to have him for all eternity—to offer him a permanent position in Heaven. Manifesting as an eagle, Zeus swoops down on Ganymede and carries him up to Olympus…*

ZEUS   &
                GANYMEDE

My dear Ganymede, we have come to our journey's
end. Kiss me, you fine little fellow! There, you see I
have no crooked beak now, no sharp claws and no
wings.

> What? How? Then were you not the eagle that just
> now came flying down, and carried me away from the
> midst of my flock? But where did you get your wings?
> And how is it that you look quite different now?

Because, my brave boy, I am neither a man nor an
eagle, but the king of the gods. I only put on the form
of an eagle because it was convenient for my plans.

> What's that you say? Then you are Pan, of whom I
> have heard so much? But where is your pipe? And
> why have you no horns and no goat's feet?

Did you think that there are no gods but him?

> In our village, we know of no other; therefore we
> sacrifice to him a whole he-goat before the cave where
> his image stands. Maybe you are one of those bad
> men who steal folks, and then sell them for slaves!

Tell me, have you never heard talk of Zeus, and never
seen on the top of Ida the altar of the god who sends
rain and lightning and thunder?

Oh—then you are the fine gentleman that lately pelted us so terribly with all those hailstones; who, as they say, lives up in the sky, and who makes such a clattering among the clouds, and to whom my father only a few days ago sacrificed a ram? But what have I done, that you should thus fly away with me, o king of the gods? My sheep will be running wild by now, and are perhaps already worried and torn by the wolves.

Why should you trouble yourself about the sheep?
You are now immortal, and will stay with us.

Then you will not carry me back to Ida?

Certainly not.

But my father will be angry with me, if he cannot find me anywhere, and I shall be beaten for having left my sheep.

He shall not see you again.

No, I must return to my father! If you will carry me back, I promise you, he shall sacrifice to you another ram; the big three-year old one, that always goes at the head of the flock when I drive them to the meadow.

My dear perfect Ganymede, you must drive all these things out of your head, and think no more about Ida and your flock. You are now an inmate of Heaven. Instead of milk and cheese you will eat ambrosia and drink nectar. You shall be my cup-bearer; and what is better, you will be no longer a man, but an immortal;

and a star of your name shall sparkle in the sky. You
will be quite happy.

> But when I want to play, who will be my playfellow?
> On Ida I had a great many boys of my own age...

You will be in no want of them here; I shall find you
lots of lovely playthings, and Eros shall be your play-
fellow. Take heart, my boy! Put on a cheerful face,
and never fret about things below.

> But of what service can I be to you here? Shall I have
> some sheep to look after?

Not at all. You will hand us the nectar, and wait at
table.

> Oh, there is no difficulty in that; I understand very
> well how to serve out the milk.

Will you forget about shepherding! You are in
Heaven, and here we gods drink nothing but nectar.

> Does nectar taste better than milk?

When you have tasted just one drop of it, you will no
longer wish for milk.

> But where am I to sleep at night? With my compan-
> ion Eros?

Little numbskull, I brought you away that you may
sleep with me!

You have trouble sleeping alone, and imagine that
you shall sleep sounder if you lie with me?

With such a pretty boy as you, certainly.

What has prettiness to do with sleeping?

Oh, it has something dreamy in it, and makes one
sleep softer!

My father thinks differently. He was always kept
awake by me when I lay with him; and complained
in the morning that I was always tossing about, and
rolling this way and that, and would kick him, or
cry out in my sleep, so that he could get no rest for
me; and therefore generally sent me to bed with my
mother. If you stole me for that, you can carry me
back to the earth; for I shall be very troublesome to
you, as I turn so often.

So much the better. I warrant we shall find something to talk about.

But I shall be asleep…

We shall see what is to be done. In the meantime—
Hermes, take him away for now, and let him drink
the draught of immortality. Then show him how he
must offer the goblet with propriety; when he has
learned, bring him back so that he may begin his new
career at table.

7   "I thought it was just the women and the girls that made you cross."

What a lot ZEUS' wife has to put up with. These days he can barely be trusted in his desire for more and lovelier playmates—and now he has promoted his latest, the boy Ganymede, to immortality. Not only that, but the king of the gods has made him Heavenly cup-bearer, sacking Hera's son Hephaestus from the role. Confronting Zeus and Ganymede together, HERA makes her feelings plain. Zeus brazens it out; Ganymede stands meekly by in silence...

HERA   &
                       ZEUS

Ever since you brought up this Phrygian boy from
Ida, I find you grown very cold towards me, Zeus.

                    You are jealous of this simple, harmless lad? I thought
                    it was just the women and girls that made you cross.

It is unbecoming of you. And, I might add, ill befits
the dignity of the king of the gods to neglect your
lawful wife, and to carry on your intrigues below,
rambling about the earth in the shape of a swan, or
a bull, or a satyr. But at least the creatures stay where
they belong—unlike this shepherd-boy, to your
eternal disgrace, who you have even fetched up into
Heaven, and settled him here before my face, under
the pretext of handing you your nectar. As if you
were at a loss for a cup-bearer, and Hephaestus were
no longer able to cope with so arduous an office! To
make matters worse, you never take the goblet from
his hand, but give him a kiss before the eyes of us all,
which tastes to you sweeter than the nectar, so that
you are every moment asking for drink, though you
are not thirsty. You even carry it so far that when you
have only drunk a little, you hand the cup to the boy
and make him drink, that you may gulp down what
he leaves, as if the dregs were something peculiarly
delicious; putting always that part of the brim to your
mouth which he has touched with his lips, that you
may have the pleasure of drinking and kissing at

once, I suppose. And did you not the other day lay
aside your aegis and your thunderbolt, in despite of
your dignity and your great long beard, to sit down on
the ground and play with him? Do not imagine that
I don't notice these things; I see it all perfectly well.

> And where is the harm in all this, my lady wife, if,
> to take a double pleasure from my cups, I kiss such
> a pretty boy? If I allowed him only once to kiss you,
> you would not find fault with me, but would be very
> well content, and prefer his kiss to the nectar.

Zeus! I hope never to proceed so far in condescension as to let my lips be contaminated by a Phrygian
shepherd-boy—and such an effeminate stripling too!

> Mind your language, madam—this effeminate
> stripling, this Phrygian shepherd-boy, this delicate
> youth…Ah, goodness, I had best say no more, lest I
> overheat myself!

Oh, for anything I have to say about it, you may as
well be married to him! I only said it to put you in
mind of the improprieties you force me to endure on
account of your cup-bearer.

> So! Your delicate son, Hephaestus, smutty and be-
> grimed with coal-dust as he comes from his forge,
> should therefore limp about the celestial table and
> serve us out the wine? From such fingers you think
> we ought to take the cup, and be glad of it? We
> should content ourselves with his sooty kisses, with
> which you yourself are disgusted, though you are his

mother? That would be delightful! Oh, that would be a cup-bearer highly ornamental to the celestial table! Ganymede must be sent back to Ida; for he is cleanly, and has rosy fingers, and hands the goblet with a grace; and, what vexes you the most, kisses sweeter than nectar!

It is only since you brought up this fine curly-haired rustic that Hephaestus is all at once become crippled, and powdered over with ashes, and so shocking a sight to you! Formerly you saw nothing of all this, and neither his soot nor his forge prevented you from relishing the nectar presented you from his hands.

Dear Hera, you vex only yourself. That is all you get by your jealousy; my love for you is only strained the higher for it. If, however, it is disagreeable to you to take your cup from the hand of a beautiful boy, then so be it—let it be presented to you by your son. And you, Ganymede, shall in future wait upon me alone; and with every cup kiss me twice when you hand it to me, and when you take it back— What? Why do you cry, child? Don't you worry; I swear, whoever has upset you shall suffer for it!

8

"Whew! I have a rival, I find;
and with my own lawful wife."

Down on earth, Ixion, king of the ancient tribe of Lapiths, has killed his father-in-law by pushing him into a bed of burning coals. Overcome with guilt, he goes mad and is shunned by his people, forced to live as an outlaw. ZEUS (it might be said, in an uncharacteristically sentimental moment, bearing in mind that he has already seduced Ixion's wife) takes pity on him and brings him up to Heaven. But Ixion is not so easily rehabilitated; he soon takes a shine to HERA and intends to pursue her into the bedroom. What is to be done?

HERA   &
               ZEUS

Zeus! What is your opinion of this man Ixion?

> Why, my dear, I think he is a very good sort of man;
> and the best of company. Indeed, if he were unworthy
> of our company, he would not be here.

He is unworthy! He is a villain! Discard him!

> Eh? What has he been after? I must know about this.

I scarce know how to tell you. The wretch!

> Oh; if he is a wretch, you must certainly tell me all
> about it! What, has he been making advances?

And to me! To me, of all people! It has been going on
for a long time. At first, when he would keep looking
at me, I had no idea—and then he would sigh and
groan; and when I handed my cup to Ganymede after
drinking, he would insist on having it, and would
stop drinking to kiss it, and lift it up to his eyes; and
then he would look at me again. And then of course
I knew. For a long time I didn't like to say anything to
you; I thought his mad fit would pass. But when he
actually dared to speak to me, I left him weeping and
grovelling about, and stopped my ears, so that I might
not hear his impertinences, and came to tell you. It is
for you to consider what steps you will take.

Whew! I have a rival, I find; and with my own lawful
wife. Here is a rascal who has tippled his nectar to
some purpose. Well, we have no one but ourselves
to blame for it: we make too much of these mortals,
admitting them to our table like this. When they drink
of our nectar, and behold the beauties of Heaven (so
different from those of Earth!), it is no wonder if they
fall in love, and form ambitious schemes! Yes, love
is all-powerful; and not with mortals only: we gods
have sometimes fallen beneath its sway.

He has made himself master of you; no doubt of
that. He does what he likes with you—leads you by
the nose. You follow him whither he chooses, and
assume every shape at his command; you are his
chattel, his toy. I know how it will be: you are going
to let Ixion off, because you have had relations with
his wife; she is the mother of Pirithous.

Why, what a memory you have for these little outings
of mine! Now, my idea about Ixion is this. It would
never do to punish him, or to exclude him from our
table; that would not look good. No; as he is so fond
of you, so hard hit—even to weeping point, you tell
me—

Zeus! What are you going to say?

Don't be alarmed. Let us make a cloud-phantom
in your likeness, and after dinner, as he lies awake
(which of course he will do, being in love), let us take
it and lay it by his side. It will put him out of his pain:
he will fancy he has attained his desire.

Never! The presumptuous villain!

> Yes, I know. But what harm can it do to you, if Ixion
> makes a conquest of a phantom?

But he will think that I am the phantom; he will be
working his wicked will upon me for all he can tell.

> Now you are talking nonsense. The phantom is not
> Hera, and Hera is not the phantom. Ixion will be
> deceived; that is all.

Yes, but these men are all alike—they have no
delicacy. I suppose, when he goes home, he will boast
to everyone of how he has enjoyed the embraces of
Hera, the wife of Zeus! Why, he may tell them that I
am in love with him! And they will believe it; they
will know nothing about the phantom.

> If he says anything of the kind he shall soon find
> himself in Hades, spinning round on a wheel for all
> eternity. That will keep him busy! And serve him
> right; not for falling in love—I see no great harm in
> that—but for letting his tongue wag.

9

"She has put a cowherd in charge,
who is covered all over in eyes…"

ZEUS *is in a pickle. His wife, Hera, has caught him in the act—again—this time with a young girl called Io, one of Hera's own priestesses. In a jealous fit Hera turns Io into a cow and sends Argus, a giant with a hundred eyes and who never sleeps, to watch over Io in the pasture. If Zeus is to continue his affair with Io, the situation will require some cunning. He turns to* HERMES *for assistance…*

ZEUS   &
               HERMES

Hermes, you know Inachus's beautiful daughter?

                    I do. Io, you mean?

Yes; except she is not a girl now, but a cow.

                    Magic at work! How did that come about?

Hera had a jealous fit, and transformed her. But that
is not all; she has thought of a new punishment for
the poor thing. She has put a cowherd in charge, who
is covered all over in eyes; this Argus, as he is called,
pastures the cow, and never goes to sleep.

                    Well, what am I to do?

Fly down to Nemea, where the pasture is. Kill Argus,
take Io across the sea to Egypt, and convert her into Isis.
She shall henceforth be an Egyptian Goddess, flood the
Nile, regulate the winds, and rescue mariners.

10 "He has at this time a particular need for a longer night than ordinary…"

Zeus is getting craftier, bolder, and more ambitious with his trysts. He decides that Alcmene, wife of the great warrior Amphitryon, will make a fine sexual partner in his desire to create a hero for the ages. In order to allow him enough time to give of his best, he sends HERMES to speak to HELIOS, the sun god, with orders to stay in for a couple of days. This is abhorrent to Helios, who revolts at the very idea—even if it will allow for the conception of Heracles…

HERMES   &
                  HELIOS

Helios, you are not to go out today, Zeus says, nor
tomorrow, nor the day after. The whole while is to
be but one continued night. You may therefore un-
harness your horses; you are also to extinguish your
torch and rest up for the time.

> This is a strange and surprising order that you bring
> me. Does he think perhaps that I have not properly
> performed my duties, and is therefore so angry with
> me that he will in future make the night thrice as
> long as the day?

That is not the reason; neither is it always to be so:
but he has at this time a particular need for a longer
night than ordinary.

> Where is he then at present, and whence did he send
> you with this message to me?

From Boeotia, from the wife of Amphitryon, where
he is on a visit.

> That is she with whom he is in love… But would he
> not have enough of her in one night?

By no means. From this union is to spring a great
and ever victorious hero—an all conquering god,
indeed—and that can never be effected in one night.

Well, good luck to him! But—between ourselves, Hermes—in Saturn's time such things did not use to happen. *He* never forsook Rhea's bed, nor stole away from heaven to pass the night at Thebes: but day was day, and a night lasted not a minute longer than it ought to. Whereas now, for the sake of one graceless woman, all nature must be turned upside down; my horses grow restive for want of exercise, and my road more rough and difficult to travel, by lying unbeaten for three days together: poor mankind must live miserably in darkness all the while, and—thanks to the amorous temperament of the king of the gods!— there they must sit waiting in that long obscurity, till this great athlete you speak of is finished!

Silence, Helios! Your glib tongue may bring you into trouble. I must speed to Selene and to Hypnos, that I may deliver Zeus' commands to them likewise; to the former that she must march slower across the night sky, and the latter to keep the mortals fast asleep, that they may not perceive how long the night is. Farewell!

11   "That son of yours; it is he who must answer for it all…"

APHRODITE *(the great goddess of love) pops in to see* SELENE *(goddess of the moon) for a gossip—only to find that her son, Eros, has been up to his usual tricks, firing his arrows as the mood takes him and making gods fall hopelessly in love with mortals. Selene is feeling the pangs of love deeply; she is spending more and more time on earth, watching over the handsome hunter Endymion…*

APHRODITE & SELENE

What is this I hear about you, Selene? When your chariot is over Caria, you stop it to gaze at Endymion sleeping hunter-fashion in the open; sometimes, they tell me, you actually get out and go down to him.

> Ah, Aphrodite, ask that son of yours; it is he who must answer for it all.

Well now, what a naughty boy! He gets his own mother into all sorts of scrapes; I must go down, now to Ida for Anchises of Troy, now to Lebanon for my Assyrian stripling;—mine? No, he put Persephone in love with him too, and so robbed me of half my darling. I have told him many a time that if he would not behave himself I would break his bow for him, and clip his wings; and before now I have smacked his little behind with my slipper. It is no use; he is frightened and cries for a minute or two, and then forgets all about it. But tell me, is Endymion handsome? That is always a comfort in our humiliation.

> Most handsome, I think, my dear; you should see him when he has spread out his cloak on the rock and is asleep; his javelins in his left hand, just slipping from his grasp, the right arm bent upwards, making a bright frame to the face, and he breathing softly in helpless slumber. Then I come noiselessly down, treading on tiptoe not to wake and startle him—but there, you know all about it; why tell you the rest? I am dying of love, and that is all.

12 "You wicked boy, your poor mother is quite uneasy."

APHRODITE's son, EROS, *is really running wild. His latest target is the Titan Rhea, the mother of all gods, and who is, correspondingly, extremely advanced in years. Mischievous Eros has caused her to fall in love with Attis, a young shepherd boy and devotee. Rhea, full of renewed lust and vigour, is tearing about on her lion-drawn chariot, backed by a chorus of wailing Corybantes. Aphrodite, who sees that this can only end badly, resolves to have a stiff word with her son about where he points his bow in future. But the eternal child is unrepentant...*

APHRODITE &
EROS

Child, child, you must think what you are doing.
It is bad enough on earth—you are always inciting
men to do some mischief, to themselves or to one
another—but I am speaking of the gods. You change
Zeus into shape after shape as the fancy takes you;
you make Selene come down from the sky; you keep
Helios loitering about with Clymene, till he sometimes forgets to drive out. As for the naughty tricks
you play on your own mother, you know you are safe
there. But Rhea! How could you dare to set her on
thinking of that young fellow in Phrygia, an old lady
like her, the mother of so many gods? Why, you have
made her quite mad: she harnesses those lions of
hers, and drives about all over Ida with the Corybantes, who are as mad as herself, shrieking high and
low for Attis; and there they are, slashing their arms
with swords, rushing about over the hills, like wild
things, with dishevelled hair, blowing horns, beating
drums, clashing cymbals; all Ida is one mad tumult.
I am quite uneasy about it; yes, you wicked boy, your
poor mother is quite uneasy: some day when Rhea
is in one of her mad fits (or when she is in her senses,
more likely), she will send the Corybantes after you,
with orders to tear you to pieces, or throw you to the
lions. You are too venturesome!

Be under no alarm, mother; I understand lions
perfectly. I get on to their backs every now and then,

and take hold of their manes, and ride them about; and when I put my hand into their mouths, they only lick it, and let me take it out again. Besides, how is Rhea going to have time to attend to me? She is too busy with Attis. And I see no harm in just pointing out beautiful things to people; they can leave them alone—it is nothing to do with me. And how would you like it if Ares were not in love with you, or you with him?

Masterful boy! Always the last word! But you will remember this some day.

13 "Are you still brooding over that affair of Daphne?"

Poor APOLLO—his passion for the nymph Daphne came to a sudden end when her father turned her into a tree in order to protect her virtue; now he is grieving for his latest love, the young prince Hyacinth, whom he has inadvertently killed in a game of quoits. He flies to HERMES seeking wisdom and sympathy. But Hermes' response is characteristically pragmatic…

HERMES &
APOLLO

Why so sad, Apollo?

                    Alas, Hermes—my love!

Oh; that's bad. What, are you still brooding over that
affair of Daphne?

                    No. I grieve for my beloved; the Laconian, the son
                    of Oebalus.

Hyacinth? He is not dead?

                    Dead.

Who killed him? Who could have the heart? That
lovely boy!

                    It was the work of my own hand.

You must have been mad!

                    Not mad; it was an accident.

Oh? How did it happen?

                    He was learning to throw the quoit, and I was throw-
                    ing with him. I had just sent my quoit up into the air
                    as usual, when jealous Zephyr (damned be he above

all winds! He had long been in love with Hyacinth, though Hyacinth would have nothing to say to him) came blustering down from Taygetus, and dashed the quoit upon the child's head; blood flowed from the wound in streams, and in one moment all was over. My first thought was of revenge; I lodged an arrow in Zephyr, and pursued his flight to the mountain. As for the child, I buried him at Amyclae, on the fatal spot; and from his blood I have caused a flower to spring up, sweetest, fairest of flowers, inscribed with letters of woe. Is my grief unreasonable?

It is, Apollo. You knew that you had set your heart upon a mortal: grieve not then for his mortality.

14

"Running with sweat and all sooty-faced; and yet they cuddle and kiss him!"

HERMES *and* APOLLO *aren't feeling very lucky in love. This in contrast with the apparently miraculous achievements of the blacksmith Hephaestus who, despite being rather rough and ready, has taken two lovely wives—one in Heaven (Aphrodite), and one on earth (the celebrated beauty Charis). United in their envy, they meet to discuss this uneven state of affairs…*

HERMES &
          APOLLO

To think that a cripple and a blacksmith like Hephaestus should marry two such queens of beauty as
Aphrodite and Charis!

> Luck, Hermes—that is all. But I do wonder at their
> putting up with his company; they see him running
> with sweat, bent over the forge, all sooty-faced; and
> yet they cuddle and kiss him, and sleep with him!

Yes, it makes me angry too; how I envy him! Ah,
Apollo, you may let your locks grow, and play your
harp, and be proud of your looks; I am a healthy
fellow, and can pluck the lyre; but, when it comes to
bedtime, we lie alone.

> Well, my loves never prosper; Daphne and Hyacinth
> were my great passions; she so detested me that
> being turned into a tree was more attractive than I;
> and him I killed with a quoit. Nothing is left of them
> but wreaths of their leaves and flowers.

Ah, once, I and Aphrodite—but no; no boasting.

> I know; that is how Hermaphroditus is accounted
> for. But perhaps you can tell me how it is that Aphro-
> dite and Charis are not jealous of one another.

Because one is his wife in Lemnos and the other in
Heaven. Besides, Aphrodite cares most about Ares;
he is her real love; so she does not trouble her head
about the blacksmith.

                     Do you think Hephaestus knows?

Oh, he knows; but what can he do? He also knows
what a martial young fellow Ares is, so he holds his
tongue. He talks of inventing a net, though, to take
them in the act with.

                     All I know is, I would not mind being taken in that
                     act!

15 "Madam; we cannot all be the proud mothers of Hephaestuses."

HERA *and* LETO *discuss their respective children by Zeus. Hera has rough Hephaestus, the crippled blacksmith and Olympian armourer; Leto has both the multi-talented Apollo, and Artemis, the wild and comely hunter. Leto thinks Hera a stuck-up and cuckolded nag; Hera thinks Leto a bimbo, with children no better. And they go on from there…*

HERA   &
                   LETO

I must congratulate you, madam, on the children
with whom you have presented Zeus.

> Ah, madam; we cannot all be the proud mothers
> of Hephaestuses.

My boy may be a cripple, but at least he is of some
use. He is a wonderful smith, and has made Heaven
look another place; and Aphrodite thought him
worth marrying, and dotes on him still. But those
two of yours! That girl is wild and mannish to a
degree; and now she has gone off to Scythia, and
her doings there are no secret; she is as bad as any
Scythian herself, butchering strangers and eating
them! Apollo, too, who pretends to be so clever,
with his bow and his lyre and his medicine and his
prophecies; those oracle-shops that he has opened
at Delphi, and Clarus, and Dindyma, are a cheat;
he takes good care to be on the safe side by giving
ambiguous answers that no one can understand, and
makes money out of it, for there are plenty of fools
who like being imposed upon—but sensible people
know well enough that most of it is clap-trap. The
prophet did not know that he was to kill his favourite
with a quoit; he never foresaw that Daphne would
run away from him, so handsome as he is, too, such
beautiful hair! I am not sure, after all, that there is
much to choose between your children and Niobe's.

Oh, of course; my children are butchers and impostors. I know how you hate the sight of them. You cannot bear to hear my girl complimented on her looks, or my boy's playing admired by the company.

His playing, madam!—excuse a smile—why, if the Muses had not favoured him, his contest with Marsyas would have cost him his skin; poor Marsyas was shamefully used on that occasion; 'twas a judicial murder. As for your charming daughter, when Actaeon once caught sight of her charms, she had to set the dogs upon him, for fear he should tell all he knew: I forbear to ask where the innocent child picked up her knowledge of obstetrics.

You set no small value on yourself, madam, because you are the wife of Zeus, and share his throne; you may insult whom you please. But there will be tears presently, when the next bull or swan sets out on his travels, and you are left neglected again.

16 "It is a spectacle well worth seeing, I assure you!"

Sequel to their last discussion, HERMES *has news for* APOLLO: *Hephaestus, enraged at his new wife's continued passion for Ares, has finally made good on his plans to expose them…*

APOLLO &
HERMES

Something tickling you, Hermes?

>Oh—it is too much! Aphrodite and Ares are caught together in the fact, and ensnared so artfully by Hephaestus that they cannot get free yet.

How did he manage that? Do tell, for it must be a diverting story!

>He had long had his suspicions, and only waited for a favourable opportunity. Having forged a most curious net—which I lately told you about— he set it about the marital bed, and then made a fuss about some work he had to do at his forge at Lemnos. Scarcely was he gone when Ares, suspecting nothing of the trick, crept in by stealth: but he was seen by Helios, who immediately gave intelligence of it to Hephaestus. In the meantime, our lovers climbed into bed, but soon entangled themselves—you may imagine how—in the invisible meshes, which worked delightfully. All of a sudden in came Hephaestus in his proper person. The poor lady, who was in the state of simple nature, was ready to die with shame, nothing being within reach to cover herself with: for his part, Ares for a while thought he could tear the net and save himself by flight; but, finding that to be impossible, had to resort to appeal.

And Hephaestus? Did he release them?

> No; he would not let them off so easily. He called all
> the gods together, as witnesses to his happiness in
> wedlock. You can imagine the embarrassment of the
> two performers, in the muddle they were in; it is a
> spectacle well worth seeing, I assure you!

But is the blacksmith not ashamed to proclaim to all
the world his own disgrace?

> Oh, by Zeus; he stands by, and laughs louder than all
> the rest! For myself, I could not help thinking that
> Ares, when I beheld him so entangled with the fairest
> of all the goddesses, was in a very enviable situation.

You would submit to being shackled at that price?

> And you would not, Apollo? I say, come only and see
> for yourself, and if you are not at the first glance of
> my opinion, I will sing to your enlightenment.

17 "What a handful the fellow would be if he were sober."

HERA, *by now totally fed up with* ZEUS' *unceasing efforts to populate Heaven with offspring, turns her scorn onto the antics of Dionysus, Zeus' son by Semele. Is such a popinjay a worthy successor? Zeus thinks so; after all, the boy seems to have done rather well for himself…*

HERA   &
                ZEUS

Well, Zeus, I should be ashamed if I had such a son;
so effeminate, and so given to drinking; tying up his
hair in a ribbon, indeed! And spending most of his
time among mad women, himself as much a woman
as any of them; dancing to flute and drum and
cymbal! He resembles anyone other than his father.

> Anyhow, my dear, this wearer of ribbons, this
> woman among women, not content with conquering
> Lydia, subduing Thrace, and enthralling the people
> of Tmolus, has been on an expedition all the way to
> India with his womanish host, captured elephants,
> taken possession of the country, and led their king
> captive after a brief resistance. And he never stopped
> dancing all the time, never relinquished the thyrsus
> and the ivy; always drunk (as you say) and always
> inspired! If any scoffer presumes to make light of his
> ceremonial, he does not go unpunished; he is bound
> with vine-twigs; or his own mother mistakes him for
> a fawn, and tears him limb from limb. Are not these
> manful doings, worthy of a son of Zeus? No doubt
> he is fond of his comforts, too, and his amusements;
> we need not complain of that: you may judge from
> his drunken achievements, what a handful the fellow
> would be if he were sober.

I suppose you will tell me next that the invention of
wine is very much to his credit; though you see for

yourself how drunken men stagger about and mis-
behave themselves; one would think the liquor had
made them mad. Look at Icarius, the first to whom
he gave the vine: beaten to death with mattocks by
his own boon companions!

Nonsense. That is not Dionysus' fault, nor the wine's
fault; it comes of the immoderate use of it. Men will
drink their wine neat, and drink too much of it.
Taken in moderation, it engenders cheerfulness and
benevolence. Dionysus is not likely to treat any of his
guests as Icarius was treated. No; I see what it is: you
are jealous, my love; you can't forget about Semele,
and so you must disparage the noble achievements
of her son.

18 "Those awful, flashing eyes! She is like a man, only worse."

APHRODITE *is puzzled: why does* EROS, *who usually can't be stopped from sticking his magical arrows into people—often just for mischief—shy away from Athena, Zeus' daughter by his first wife Metis? What have the Muses done to deserve his reticence? And why does Artemis always seem to get away from him?*

APHRODITE   &
                 EROS

Eros, dear, you have had your victories over most of
the gods—Zeus, Poseidon, Rhea, Apollo, nay, your
own mother; how is it you make an exception for
Athena? Against her your torch has no fire, your
quiver no arrows, your right hand no cunning.

> I am afraid of her, mother; those awful flashing eyes!
> She is like a man, only worse. When I go against her
> with my arrow on the string, a toss of her plume
> frightens me; my hand shakes so that it drops the bow.

I should have thought Ares was more terrible still;
but you disarmed and conquered him.

> Ah, he is only too glad to have me; he calls me to him.
> Athena always eyes me so! Once I flew close past her,
> quite by accident, with my torch. "If you come near
> me," she called out, "I swear by my father, I will run
> you through with my spear, or take you by the foot and
> drop you into Tartarus, or tear you in pieces with my
> own hands"—and more such dreadful things. And
> she has such a sour look; and then on her breast
> she wears that horrid face with the snaky hair; that
> frightens me worst of all. I run away directly I see it.

Well, well, you are afraid of Athena and the Gorgon;
at least so you say, though you do not mind Zeus's
thunderbolt a bit. But why do you let the Muses go

scot free? Do they toss their plumes and hold out
Gorgons' heads?

> Ah, mother, they make me bashful; they are so
> grand, always studying and composing; I love to
> stand there listening to their music.

So you let them pass too, because they are grand.
And why do you never take a shot at Artemis?

> Why, the great thing is that I cannot catch her; she is
> always over the hills and far away. But besides that,
> her heart is engaged already.

Where, child?

> In hunting stags and fawns; she is so fleet, she catches
> them up, or else shoots them; she can think of noth-
> ing else. Her brother, now, though he is an archer too,
> and draws a good arrow—

I know, child—you have hit him often enough.

19

"If you don't stop, I shall soon show you that immortality is not much good."

ASCLEPIUS' and HERACLES' time on earth is done. Now that they are both in Heaven, an argument over brains versus brawn has broken out; the two heroes each believe they should take precedence at the celestial dinner table. Asclepius is blessed with an unrivalled knowledge of drugs and medicine; Heracles with unsurpassed strength and boldness. Heracles has relied on Asclepius' skill in the past, but Asclepius has been in trouble before for bringing dead people back to life. Meanwhile, ZEUS is trying to eat his dinner…

ZEUS,

ASCLEPIUS &

HERACLES

Now, Asclepius and Heracles, stop that quarrel-
ling; you might as well be men; such behaviour
is very improper and out of place at the table of
the gods.

> Is this druggist fellow to have a place above
> me, Zeus?

Of course I am; I am your better.

> Why, you numbskull? Because it was Zeus's
> bolt that cracked your skull, for your unholy
> doings, and now you have been allowed your
> immortality again out of sheer pity?

You taunt me with my fiery end; you seem to
have forgotten that you too were burnt to death,
on Oeta.

> Was there no difference between your life
> and mine, then? I am Zeus' son, and it is
> well known how I toiled, cleansing the earth,
> conquering monsters, and chastising men
> of violence. Whereas you are a root-grubber
> and a quack; I dare say you have your use for
> doctoring sick men, but you never did a bold
> deed in your life.

ZEUS,

ASCLEPIUS &
HERACLES

That comes well from you, whose burns I
healed, when you came up all singed not so
long ago; between the tunic and the flames,
your body was half consumed. Anyhow, it
would be enough to mention that I was never
a slave like you, never combed wool in Lydia,
masquerading in a purple shawl and being
slippered by an Omphale, never killed my wife
and children in a fit of the spleen.

If you don't stop being rude, I shall soon show
you that immortality is not much good. I will
take you up and pitch you head over heels out
of Heaven, and Apollo himself shall never
mend your broken crown.

Cease, I say, and let us hear ourselves speak, or
I will send you both away from table. Heracles,
Asclepius died before you, and has the right to
a better place.

20

"Mind what you say, Ares; it is not
safe to talk like that…"

*Zeus, looking down on the multitude of gods and heirs that he has sired,
has been boasting of his immaculate might. But pride often comes before
a fall—something ARES ought to know all about. The great god of war,
and eternal strategist, has done the calculations: perhaps, he queries
HERMES, the old philanderer is not quite as indomitable as he imagines?*

ARES   &
              HERMES

Did you hear Zeus' threat, Hermes? Most complimentary,
wasn't it, and most practicable? "If I choose," says he, "I could
let down a rope from Heaven, and all of you might hang on to
it and do your very best to pull me down; it would be wasted
labour; you would never move me. On the other hand, if I
chose to haul up, I should have you all dangling in mid-air,
with earth and sea into the bargain"—and so on. You heard?
Well, I dare say he is too much for any of us individually, but
I will never believe he outweighs the whole of us in body, or
that, even with the makeweight of earth and sea, we should
not get the better of him.

              Mind what you say, Ares; it is not safe to talk like that;
              we might get paid out for chattering.

You don't suppose I should say this to everyone; I am not
afraid of you; I know you can keep a quiet tongue. I must tell
you what made me laugh most while he stormed: I remember
not so long ago, when Poseidon and Hera and Athena rebelled
and made a plot for his capture and imprisonment, he was
frightened out of his wits; well, there were only three of them,
and if Thetis had not taken pity on him and called in the hun-
dred-handed Briareus to the rescue, he would actually have
been put in chains, with his thunder and his bolt beside him.
When I worked out the sum, I could not help laughing.

              Oh, do be quiet; such things are too risky for you to
              say or me to listen to.

21 "How should I come by a son with horns, and a tail at his rump?"

It seems that HERMES' *past has caught up with him:* PAN, *the goaty god of nature and companion of the nymphs, is claiming Hermes as his father. Hermes can't recall the liaison that resulted in Pan's issue—but a tacit acknowledgment might just have its advantages…*

PAN   &
                       HERMES

Good-day, father Hermes!

> Oh, good-day to you likewise! But since when are we
> such close relations?

Are you not then Hermes of Cyllene?

> Certainly I am; but how then does it follow that you
> are my son?

Not quite regularly—but the natural offspring of love,
after your fashion.

> By Zeus, you look more like the son of a she-goat,
> after the fashion of a he-goat. How should I come by
> a son with horns, and with such a nose and such a
> shaggy beard and cloven feet, and a tail at his rump?

In speaking so scornfully of me, you dishonour us
both; I am just as you made me; I cannot help my form.

> Who was then your mother? I hope I have not un-
> wittingly come in contact with a she-goat.

Not at all; but recollect whether you did not once
seduce a free-born maid in Arcadia? Why do you bite
your nails, and make as if you could not call it to mind?
I speak of the daughter of Icarius, Penelope.

But what sort of fancy was that, to present me with a son resembling a goat?

I will tell you how she herself related the affair. When she sent me to Arcadia, she said to me: 'My son, I your mother am Penelope of Sparta: but know that you have a god for your father—Hermes, the son of Zeus and Maia. Let it not trouble you that you have horns and goat's feet, for Hermes, in order not to be discovered, assumed the form of a goat when he became your father.'

Something of the kind may have once happened. But that I, who have always prided myself on my figure, and have a smooth chin, should pass for your father, and be laughed at by everybody for my beautiful offspring—this I cannot easily digest.

I shall be no disgrace to you, father; I am a musician, and play upon the pipe to admiration; and Dionysus, who cannot live without me, has taken me for his constant companion, and made me leader of his band. And if you were to see the flocks which I have about Tegea and mount Parthenius, it would be a real pleasure to you. All Arcadia is subject to me; and not so long ago I marched to reinforce the Athenians with my succours, and behaved so well at Marathon that they have granted me the cavern beneath the citadel as a reward for my bravery. If ever you should go to Athens, you will hear what a great name Pan has acquired there.

Indeed? Since, then, you are a person of so much consequence, Pan—for so you call yourself—have you managed to take a wife?

Thanks, honoured father! But I am of rather a warm
temperament, and should not be content with just
one.

> You are very great then, I imagine, with the goats?

It pleases you to be witty. Oh, I have different affairs
of gallantry! With Echo, Peitho, and all the Maenads
of Dionysus, numerous as they are, and I am very
much valued by them, I can assure you.

> Indeed…Well—son!—will you then grant me one
> favour? Come hither and embrace me! But just one
> thing: be sure never to call me father when anybody
> is within earshot…

22 "I must tell you something very diverting about Priapus…"

APOLLO *is baffled by the natures of Aphrodite's three children. There is Eros, the eternal child who, with his bow and arrow, has the power to make people fall instantly in love; there is Hermaphroditus, who is neither male nor female—or is both, depending on one's point of view; and finally there is the gigantically over-endowed, and permanently aroused, Priapus. Talking of whom,* DIONYSUS *has a tale to tell…*

APOLLO   &
               DIONYSUS

Who would believe, Dionysus, that Eros, Hermaphroditus, and Priapus, were all brothers? They, who in
form, temper, and manners are so very unlike! For
the first is everything that can be called beautiful,
and expert in handling the bow, and is endowed with
a power whereby he is master of all the world. The
second is effeminate, only a portion of a man, with
such an ambiguous countenance, that at first sight
it is difficult to decide whether he is a boy or a girl;
whereas Priapus is more of a man than he should be.

> That is not so surprising as you may think, Apollo;
> Aphrodite is not to be blamed for it, but the differ-
> ence of the fathers. It happens sometimes, that the
> same mother has by one father twins of different
> sexes, as was the case with you and Artemis.

That may perhaps be true: but we are alike, and follow
the same employment; for we are both archers.

> That is as far as the resemblance goes: for Artemis
> slays strangers among the Scythians; whereas you are
> a prophet and a physician.

Think not that my sister is so delighted with these
Scythians! She so much abhors these massacres, that
she has made up her mind to go away with the first
Grecian that chance shall bring to Tauris.

        There she is right! But to return to Priapus, of whom
        I must tell you something very diverting. Lately hap-
        pening to be at Lampsacus, I took up my quarters with
        him; he gave me the best entertainment his means
        could afford, and at length we retired to rest, after a
        plentiful evening's carousing. About midnight my
        noble host rose up, and—I am ashamed to proceed…

I understand. And what did you do?

        What should I do? I laughed at him!

That was right of you, not to take the matter too
seriously, and make a noise about it. It was pardon-
able of him to try his luck with one so handsome as
you are.

        He would have had more reason to do you so much
        honour, Apollo; your beauty and your golden locks
        would have pleaded his excuse.

He would not be greatly inclined towards me: I wear
besides my fine curls a bow and arrow.

23 "Am I to do all the work of Heaven with my own hands?"

It is said that talent is its own reward. HERMES *may be the most talented lad in Heaven, but as he confides to his mother,* MAIA, *even a god of his energies and abilities may begin to feel put-upon. Such are the penalties for being a prodigy…*

HERMES   &
                  MAIA

Mother, I am the most miserable god in Heaven.

                    Don't say such things, child.

Am I to do all the work of Heaven with my own
hands, to be hurried from one piece of drudgery to
another, and never say a word? I have to get up early,
sweep the dining-room, lay the cushions and put all
to rights; then I have to wait on Zeus, and take his
messages, up and down, all day long; and I am no
sooner back again (with no time for a wash) than
I have to lay the table; and there was the nectar to
pour out, too, till this new cup-bearer was brought
in. And it really is too bad, that when everyone else
is in bed, I should have to go off to Pluto with the
Shades, and play the usher in Rhadamanthus's court.
It is not enough that I must be busy all day in the
wrestling-ground and the Assembly and the schools
of rhetoric, the dead must have their share in me
too. Leda's sons take turn and turn about betwixt
Heaven and Hades—I have to be in both every day.
And why should the sons of Alemena and Semele,
paltry women, why should they feast at their ease,
and I—the son of Maia, the grandson of Atlas—wait
upon them? And now here am I only just back from
Sidon, where he sent me to see after Europa, and
before I am in breath again—off I must go to Argos,
in quest of Danae, "and you can take Boeotia on your

way," says father, "and see Antiope." I am half dead
with it all. Mortal slaves are better off than I am: they
have the chance of being sold to a new master; I wish
I had the same!

                      Come, come, child. You must do as your father bids
                      you, like a good boy. Run along now to Argos and
                      Boeotia; don't loiter, or you will get a whipping.
                      Lovers are apt to be hasty.

24 "What have you been about, you villainous Titan? You have utterly done for the earth!"

ZEUS *is furious.* HELIOS *the sun-god, who ushers in the dawn each morning, has allowed his young son, Phaethon, to talk him into having a go in his solar chariot. The result is a calamity, a car crash of cosmic magnitude. Seeing this drama unfold, and with the earth in danger of being utterly burned up, Zeus has slain Phaethon with a thunderbolt. Crisis averted, he gives Helios a piece of his mind...*

ZEUS   &
            HELIOS

What have you been about, you villainous Titan? You
have utterly done for the earth, trusting your car to
a silly boy like that; he has got too near and scorched
it in one place, and in another killed everything with
frost by withdrawing the heat too far; there is not a
single thing he has not turned upside down. If I had
not seen what was happening and upset him with the
thunderbolt, there would not have been a remnant of
mankind left. A pretty deputy driver!

>I was wrong, Zeus; but do not be angry with me; my
>boy pressed me so. How could I tell it would turn out
>so badly?

Oh, of course you didn't know what a delicate business it is, and how the slightest divergence ruins
everything! It never occurred to you that the horses
are spirited, and want a tight hand! Oh no! Why, give
them their heads for a moment, and they are out of
control; just what happened: they carried him now
left, now right, now clean round backwards, and up
or down, just at their own sweet will. He was utterly
helpless.

>I knew it all; I held out for a long time and told him
>he mustn't drive. But he wept and entreated, and
>his mother Clymene joined in, and at last I gave in.
>I showed him how to stand, and how far he was to

mount upwards, and where to begin descending, and how to hold the reins, and keep the spirited beasts under control; and I told him how dangerous it was, if he did not keep the track. But, poor boy, when he found himself in charge of all that fire, and looking down into yawning space, he was frightened, and no wonder; and the horses soon knew I was not behind them, took the child's measure, left the track, and wrought all this havoc; he let go the reins— I suppose he was afraid of being thrown out—and held on to the rail. But he has suffered for it. My grief is punishment enough for me, Zeus.

Punishment enough, indeed! After daring to do such a thing as that! Well, I forgive you this time. But if ever you transgress again, or send another substitute like him, I will show you how much hotter the thunder-bolt is than your fire. Let his sisters bury him by the Eridanus, where he was upset. They shall weep amber tears and be changed by their grief into poplars. As for you, repair the car—the axle is broken, and one of the wheels crushed—put the horses to and drive yourself. And let this be a lesson to you.

25 "I am always calling Pollux Castor, and Castor Pollux…"

Identical twins Castor and Pollux are causing some confusion in Heaven. It's complicated: while they share a mother, Castor's father is Tyndareus, a mortal—and so he is mortal; whereas Pollux's father is Zeus—making him immortal. Now that Castor has died, Pollux has shared his immortality with him, so that they might not be parted. It's a conundrum alright: under the rules of this alternate immortality, both cannot be in Heaven at the same time—one must always be in Hades, with the dead. APOLLO is understandably perplexed and turns to HERMES for clarification…

APOLLO   &
                 HERMES

Hermes, have you any idea which of those two is
Castor, and which is Pollux? I never can make them
out.

> It was Castor yesterday, and Pollux today.

How do you tell? They are exactly alike.

> Why, Pollux's face is scarred with the wounds he got
> in boxing; those that Amycus, the Bebrycian, gave
> him, when he was on that expedition with Jason, are
> particularly noticeable. Castor has no marks; his face
> is all right.

Good; I am glad I know that. Everything else is the
same for both. Each has his half egg-shell, with the
star on top, each his javelin and his white horse. I am
always calling Pollux Castor, and Castor Pollux. And,
by the way, why are they never both here together?
Why should they be alternately gods and shades?

> That is their brotherly way. You see, it was decreed
> that one of the sons of Leda must die, and the other
> be immortal; and by this arrangement they split the
> immortality between them.

Rather a stupid way of doing it: if one of them is to
be in Heaven, whilst the other is underground, they

will never see one another at all; and I suppose that is just what they wanted to do. Then again: all the other gods practise some useful profession, either here or on earth; for instance, I am a prophet, Asclepius is a doctor, you are a first-rate gymnast and trainer, Artemis ushers children into the world; now what are these two going to do? Surely two such great fellows are not to have a lazy time of it?

> Oh no. Their business is to wait upon Poseidon, and ride the waves; and if they see a ship in distress, they go aboard of her, and save the crew.

A most humane profession.

APPENDICES

APPENDIX (i)
Historical Editions in English

The following pages contain facsimile extracts from five historical editions of Lucian published in English: John Carr's of 1773; Thomas Francklin's of 1780; William Tooke's of 1820; Howard Williams' of 1888; and Henry and Frank Fowler's of 1905. For the purposes of comparison, I have selected the same dialogue, *Eros & Zeus*, from each.

It is worth providing a brief survey of these books as they vary so much in style and content. Of the eighteenth-century editions, John Carr's *Dialogues of Lucian* (1773) is a selected works in which the *Dialogues of the Dead, of the Gods, of the Sea-Gods* and several others are shuffled about so that there is no sense of them being discrete collections.[1] The result makes for a rather disjointed read, though it is possibly a more accurate representation of Lucian's modus operandi. For all that the translation is earthy and jolly, favouring the pleasures of the common reader over the expectations of the scholar.

In stark contrast, Francklin's *Works of Lucian* (1780) might be read both as a riposte and a return to scholarship. It is certainly more respectable and much more extensive, though Francklin determinedly rejects Lucian's authorship of the bawdy *Dialogues of the Courtesans*, and leaves it aside. Unlike Carr, Francklin does separate *Dialogues of the Dead*—but conflates, perhaps quite logically, *of the Gods* and *of the Sea-Gods*. He also makes use of some helpful short introductions to each section, written in an informal, familiar style. Unhappily, it is also memorable for its ludicrous introduction, which takes the form of an imagined dialogue between Lucian—long-deceased and pottering around Elysium—and Lord Lyttleton, who has recently arrived there.

1. Not uncommon when it comes to Lucian in translation. As Frank Redmond of *The Lucian of Samosata Project* puts it, until the Tooke translation of 1820, "Lucian's editors in English simply rearranged things as they saw fit." To help clear some of this up, see Appendix (ii) for a diagram which records how all the various translators and editors have re-ordered the *Dialogues of the Gods* over the years.

Embracing each other as brothers, they set about justifying, among other things, the translation that follows—Francklin even going so far as to having them agree that Lucian did not write, and could never have written, *Dialogues of the Courtesans*.[2]

Of the nineteenth-century editions, William Tooke's *Lucian of Samosata* (1820) includes extensive footnotes courtesy of the German translator Christopher Wieland. Tooke's translation of some of the titles is charming—*Dialogues of the Sea-Gods* becomes *Confabulations of the Marine Deities*—as is the translation of the texts overall, closer in style to Carr than Francklin, but with a beautifully judged respect for the merits of both the coarser and the more refined ends of Lucian's canon. Tooke also follows Francklin's lead in discarding *Dialogues of the Courtesans*.[3]

Howard Williams' *Lucian's Dialogues* (1888) is a selected works. As with the Tooke edition, Williams precedes the translation with an extensive scholarly introduction, covering all that was known about Lucian at the time; not much has been added to that biography since. Curiously, it is Tooke's translation that remains the more sprightly read despite the significant age difference—hence my decision to use it here to fill in the blanks left by the Fowlers' censor.

2. George, Lord Lyttleton had written an original text entitled *Dialogues of the Dead* some years previously. A homage to Lucian and his work of the same name, the book follows Lucian's scheme of presenting conversations between celebrities as they arrive in the afterlife, but is updated with figures taken largely from modern history. It is fun and rather good. He died in 1773, only a couple of years before Francklin's translation was completed. In the footnotes to his introduction, Francklin carefully ensures that we are pointed to the correct Lord Lyttleton—George. The contemporaneous Lord Lyttleton—Thomas—was a sponsor of Francklin's *Works of Lucian*, though thanks to his profligacy was known commonly as 'the wicked Lord Lyttleton' so as to distinguish him from his father, "the good Lord Lyttleton".

3. All this merely a symptom of eighteenth- and nineteenth-century pruderies. Although there are several works now considered by scholars to be "pseudo-Lucian", *Dialogues of the Courtesans* is not among them. Britons would have to wait until the more liberal 1920s for a complete English translation of *Dialogues of the Courtesans* to be be published. Even then, it was done so anonymously, though we now know "A. L. H." to be A. L. Hillman. As Hillman puts it in his foreword, "These dialogues can hardly be offensive to the intelligent modern; for, somehow, our own civilization is changing, and as it becomes richer and fuller, it seems to have more in common with the civilizations of antiquity."

Digital editions of all of these, as well as the Fowler translation, are available online via *The Lucian of Samosata Project*: www.lucianofsamosata.info/resources.html.

A final note on the design of these pages: in comparing the various layouts, readers will probably find that, as with the translations themselves, they instinctively prefer one over the others. Such is the occult business of the typographic designer: their aim is to bring their skill and judgement to the composition of a page of text into which the reader will automatically and unthinkingly immerse themselves, so that they may absorb the content without ever once thinking how it might have been presented otherwise. It is only by deliberate comparison, such as is afforded here, that the reader might start to suspect that the art of considerate typographic design may directly affect their enjoyment of a text. In the words of designer Astrid Stavro, "Is a lifetime spent in details that no one will ever notice a waste? If it were, culture as we know it would simply not exist."

Dialogues of Lucian
trans. John Carr
W. Flexney, 1773

[209]

CUPID and JUPITER.

C U P I D.

I F I have been guilty of any offence, I hope, Jupiter, you will forgive me; as you fee I am a poor little boy, not come to years of dif-cretion.

J U P I T E R.

A little boy indeed! you are older than [*p*] Iapetus. You are well experienced in every fpecies of mifchief. But, becaufe your beard is not grown, nor your temples covered with fnow, truly you muft pretend to be an infant!

C U P I D.

But what harm have I done you, Jupiter? Suppofe I am old and crafty, furely I have given you no reafon for wanting to confine me?

[*p*] The fon of Titan and Terra, and the father of Prome-theus. Though the Greeks confidered him as the founder of their nation, they did not always think themfelves obliged to fpeak with refpect of him, but ufed to call any old fellow, who had outlived his faculties, Iapetus.

Cupid, according to Hefiod, is the moft ancient of the Gods. Theog. 120.

Vol. II.   J U.

JUPITER.

You little villain! you have given me reasons in abundance. Have not you made a fool of me a thousand times over? You have done with me whatever you pleased. You have metamorphosed me into a satyr, a bull, a shower of gold, a swan, an eagle, and every thing else that is ridiculous. I may well say ridiculous, for I never had a mistress that entertained any real regard for me. All your art in that has proved insufficient. To stratagem and disguise I owe all I can boast. As a bull or a swan they may endure me; but should Jupiter declare himself openly, they would all be ready to drop down dead with fear.

CUPID.

No wonder of that. What mortal can bear the aspect of Jove?

JUPITER.

How did Branchus and Hyacinthus endure Apollo?

CUPID.

Apollo need not brag; for all his fine hair and his smock face, Daphne ran away from

him

him as faft as her legs could carry her. But I will tell you what, Jupiter; if you wifh to be liked by the women, you muft not go fhaking that [*q*] ugly fhield of yours; nor rattling about your frightful thunder. Make yourfelf as pretty a fellow as you can. Do up your hair in the moft elegant tafte. Hang down a curl on each fide of your head. Wear a fine bonnet over your locks. Get a purple coat, and a pair of embroidered flippers. Trip lightly along to the found of the pipe and the timbrel. Do this, and you fhall foon have admirers more in number than the Mænades of Bacchus.

JUPITER.

Pfhaw! Do you think I would purchafe love on any fuch terms?

CUPID.

Then you muft live without love; that is all.

[*q*] Jupiter's fhield, or ægis, fo called from being covered with the fkin of the goat that fuckled him, had on it the figure of a Gorgon's head, with curling ferpents inftead of hair, fo terrible as to turn all beholders into ftone.

O 2　　　　　　　JU-

212 DIALOGUES OF LUCIAN.

JUPITER.

No, not fo neither; but I can purchafe it at an eafier rate. Go, go, get you gone.

APOLLO and VULCAN.

VULCAN.

PRAY, Apollo, have you feenMaia's hopeful brat? He is a mighty fine child, it feems; fmiles on every body, and promifes fair, they fay, to turn out fomething very extraordinary.

APOLLO.

A fine child! do you call him? He may turn out fomething very extraordinary, I grant you, for in mifchief he is already as old as the oldeft.

VULCAN.

He cannot have done any mifchief as yet, for he is but juft born.

APOLLO.

Neptune, whofe trident he has ftolen, I believe, will tell you a different tale. Or, if you

2   enquire

The Works of Lucian
trans. Thomas Francklin
T. Cadell, 1780

D I A L O G U E S OF THE G O D S. 93

think me worthy of belief, and that I can foretel what will happen here-
after?

J U P I T E R.

Moſt undoubtedly.

P R O M E T H E U S.

You are going then to Thetis, on a little intrigue with her.

J U P I T E R.

What more? for you ſeem to have hit upon the truth.

P R O M E T H E U S.

Jupiter, have nothing to do with that Nereid, for if ſhe has a child by
you, he will ſerve you as you did Saturn.

J U P I T E R.

And ſhall I be dethroned, ſayeſt thou?

P R O M E T H E U S.

Heaven forbid! But an affair with her threatens ſomething like it.

J U P I T E R.

Then, Thetis, farewel. For this advice Vulcan ſhall ſet you free.

D I A L O G U E   XXIV.

J U P I T E R AND C U P I D.

J U P I T E R.

IF I have offended, Jupiter, forgive me; I am but a poor ſimple child.

J U P I T E R.

You a child, that are * older than Japetus! becauſe you have not a beard,
and grey hairs, you would be thought a boy, as old and cunning as you are.

C U P I D.

Old as I am, as you ſay, what injury have I done you, that you ſhould
threaten to chain me?

J U P I T E R.

Why, you wicked rogue, conſider what you have done; have not you
made a laughing-ſtock of me? have not you turned me into a ſatyr, a bull,
a bit of gold, a ſwan, an eagle, and what not? but not a creature have you
inſpired with the love of me, not even ſo much as my wife. I am forced to

---

* *Older than Japetus,*] According to Heſiod (ſee his Theogony) Love was the oldeſt of all
the Gods, ſprung from Chaos, and coeval with Earth and Heaven.

make

make ufe of ftratagems to get poffeffion of them, and to difguife myfelf: they are fond of the Bull, or the Swan, perhaps ; but when I appear in my own fhape, are ready to die with fear.

C U P I D.

And well they may ; mere mortals cannot bear the fight of Jove.

J U P I T E R.

How came Apollo to be fo much beloved by Branchus and Hyacinthus ?

C U P I D.

Daphne, however, ran away from him, though he had fuch fine locks, and no beard ; but if you want to be amiable, you muft not fhake your dreadful ægis, nor carry your thunder with you, but make yourfelf as agreeable as you can ; let your hair down of each fide, and tie it with a ribbon ; wear a purple veft, put on your gold fandals, and walk in meafured pace to the found of tabor and pipe : then will you be followed by the women, as Bacchus was by the Mænades, and have as many after you.

J U P I T E R.

Away with you ; I would not wifh to be loved on fuch conditions.

C U P I D.

Then you muft not fall in love, Jupiter ; that is eafily fettled.

J U P I T E R.

Not fo neither ; I muft be in love, and happy in it, but at a cheaper rate ; and on that account you are free.

D I A L O G U E XXV.

J U P I T E R AND G A N Y M E D E.

J U P I T E R.

NOW, Ganymede, for we are come to our journey's end, kifs me ; you will find, I have no crooked beak, or fharp talons, or wings, as I had when I put on the appearance of a bird.

G A N Y M E D E.

Were not you an eagle juft now ? and did not you fly down and take me up from the midft of my flock ? and now you are a man ; your wings are off, and you feem quite another creature.

I U P I T E R,

Lucian of Samosata
trans. William Tooke
Longman, Hurst, Rees, Orme and Brown, 1820

II.

JUPITER'S COMPLAINTS AGAINST CUPID.

——————

JUPITER. CUPID.

Cupid. If I have done wrong, forgive me; I am but a simple child.

Jupiter. You a child; and yet older than Iapetus *! How! because you have neither a beard nor a grey head, you would fain pass for a boy; and yet are so old and full of roguery!

Cupid. But old as you say I am, what harm have I done you, that you threaten to chain me?

Jupiter. Is it a trifling matter then, you graceless booby, merely from perverseness and for your own diversion to have made all manner of things of me? Is not it entirely owing to you, that not a single mortal has an affection for me; so that I am at a loss what to employ against them but magic, and must turn myself into a satyr, into a bull, into an eagle, and into a golden shower †, if I would come at them. And what do I gain by it? They love the bull or the swan; but die with fright when I appear in my proper shape.

Cupid. That is very natural: how, being only mortals, should they be able to bear the sight of Jupiter?

———————————————————————————————

* That is, according to the celestial genealogy of Hesiod, whereby Cupid is as old as Chaos and the Earth, the mother of Iapetus and the other Titans, of whom Cronos or Saturn, Jupiter's father, was the youngest.

† Into a bull with Europa, into a satyr with Antiope, into a swan with Leda, into a golden shower with Danae. He might have considerably increased the catalogue; for, besides the aforesaid fair ones, he deluded Io as a cloud, Calisto as Diana, Ægina as fire, Mnemosyne as a shepherd, Clytoria as an ant, Asteria as an eagle, his sister and subsequent wife Juno as a lapwing, and Alcmene in the form of her own husband.

JUPITER. How comes it then to pass that Apollo won the affection of Branchus * and Hyacinthus?

CUPID. Daphne however ran away from him, notwithstanding he had a smooth chin and the finest head of hair in the world. If you would be loved, lay aside your lightning and that formidable ægis, make yourself as agreeable as possible, let your locks be neatly combed out, flowing in graceful ringlets on either side, ornamented with a golden fillet, put on an elegant purple vest and half-boots of gilt leather; let pipes and drums go before you; and see then whether you will not have a fairer train of nymphs than even Bacchus himself.

JUPITER. Get away with your nonsensical advice! I have no desire to be amiable at that price.

CUPID. Then neither should you desire to play the lover. That would be no hard matter.

JUPITER. Hard or not, the pleasure of love I will not renounce; I desire it to cost only little trouble. To bring that about is your affair, and on that condition you shall be pardoned for this once.

III.

I O.

JUPITER. MERCURY.

JUPITER. Mercury!

MERCURY. What are your commands, my honoured father?

---

* This Branchus was the founder of a well-known family at Mileto, under the name of the Branchides, who from their original ancestors were in possession of a very considerable oracle of Apollo Didymæus. The roman poet Statius makes him a son of Apollo. Lucian mentions him once again in the discourse on a magnificent Hall. *Branchus enim Thessalus fuit, Apollini dilectus, et filius habitus, quem interfectum dolens, templo et divinitate sacravit.* Alex. ab Alexandro, *lib. vi. cap. 2.*

Lucian's Dialogues
trans. Howard Williams
George Bell and Sons, 1888

II.

ZEUS THREATENS TO PUT EROS IN FETTERS.

Eros and Zeus.

Eros. Well, if I have really done wrong at all, Zeus, pardon me: for I am but an infant, and still without sense.

Zeus. You an infant—you the Eros, who are far older than Iapetus?[1] Because you have not grown a beard, and don't show gray hairs, do you really claim on that account to be considered an infant, when, in fact, you are an old scamp?

Eros. But what great injury have I—the old scamp, as you call me—done you, that you intend putting me in irons?

Zeus. Consider, accursed rascal, whether they are trifling injuries you have done me, you, who make such sport of me, that there is nothing which you have not turned me into—satyr, bull, gold, swan, eagle[2]—but not any one of them have you made to be in love with *me* at all; nor have I perceived that, for anything that depends upon you, I have been agreeable to any woman; but I am obliged to have recourse to juggling tricks against them, and to conceal my proper self, while they are really in love with the bull or swan, and, if they have but a glimpse of me, they die of fear.[3]

Eros. Naturally enough, Zeus, for, being mortal women, they can't endure the sight of your person.

---

[1] One of the Titans, progenitor of the human race, son of Uranus and Ge, and father of Prometheus. "As old as Iapetus" was a proverb with the Greeks, equivalent to our "as old as Adam." Cf. Hesiod Θεογ. 120; Plato Συμπ. ad init., Θ. Δ. vii. 1. and Aristoph. Νεφ. 985.

[2] An epigram in the *Greek Anthologia* thus sums up some of the principal *liaisons*, and the mistresses, of the King of Gods and Men :—

" Ζεὺς κύκνος, ταῦρος, σάτυρος, χρυσὸς δι' ἔρωτα
Λήδης, Εὐρώπης, 'Αντιόπης, Δανάης."

But the catalogue is incomplete. Besides these heroines, have been commemorated Io, Alkmena, Semele, Kallisto, Klytoria, Asteria, Ægina, Mnemosyne.

[3] Like Semele, the Theban princess, mother of Bacchus.

4 DIALOGUES OF THE GODS.

Zeus. How is it, then, that Branchus[1] and Hyacinthus love Apollo ?

Eros. But even from him the beauty, Daphne, fled away, for all his flowing locks and beardless chin. If you wish to be loved, don't shake your ægis, and don't take your thunderbolt with you ; but make yourself as agreeable as you can, letting down your locks on both sides of your face, and tying them up again under your coronet ; wear a fine purple dress, put on golden sandals, step along keeping time to the sounds of the pipe and cymbals, and you will see that more women will follow you than all the Mænads of Bacchus.

Zeus. Get away with you. I would not take the offer of being loved, on condition of becoming such a figure.

Eros. Then, Zeus, don't wish to love, either : that, at all events, is an easy matter.

Zeus. Not so ; but I do wish to love, and to enjoy their society in a less vexatious fashion. Upon this, and this condition alone, I let you go.

III.

ZEUS ORDERS HERMES TO SLAY ARGUS, AND TO CONDUCT IO TO EGYPT.

Zeus and Hermes.

Zeus. Hermes, you know the daughter of Inachus, the famous beauty ?

Hermes. Yes, you mean the far-famed Io.

Zeus. She is no longer a girl, but a heifer.

Hermes. Prodigious that ! But how was she transformed ?

Zeus. Hera, in a fit of jealousy, metamorphosed her,[2] and

---

[1] Son of Apollo by a lady of Miletus, from whom the Branchidæ, the guardians of the Oracle of Apollo at Miletus, who surrendered the treasures of their temple to Darius, derived their descent. For Hyacinthus see Θ. Δ. x. 11 ; and Ovid, *Metam.* x. 162-219.

[2] According to Ovid (*Metam.* i. 13-17), it was Jupiter himself who effected the metamorphosis, to save the Argive princess from the rage of Juno. Cf. Ἐναλ. Διαλ. vii.

The Works of Lucian of Samosata
trans. H. W. and F. G. Fowler
Oxford at The Clarendon Press, 1905

Zeus. Right so far. And the sequel ? I trust you now.

Prom. Have no dealings with her, Zeus. As sure as Nereus's daughter conceives by you, your child shall mete you the measure you meted to——

Zeus. I shall lose my kingdom, you would say ?

Prom. Avert it, Fate ! I say only, that union portends this issue.

Zeus. Thetis, farewell ! and for this Hephaestus shall set you free.   H.

II

' *Eros. Zeus*

Eros. You might let me off, Zeus ! I suppose it *was* rather too bad of me ; but there !—I am but a child ; a wayward child.

Zeus. A child, and born before Iapetus was ever thought of ? You bad old man ! Just because you have no beard, and no white hairs, are you going to pass yourself off for a child ?

Eros. Well, and what such mighty harm has the old man ever done you, that you should talk of chains ?

Zeus. Ask your own guilty conscience, what harm. The pranks you have played me ! Satyr, bull, swan, eagle, shower of gold,—I have been everything in my time ; and I have you to thank for it. You never by any chance make the women in love with *me* ; no one is ever smitten with *my* charms, that I have noticed. No, there must be magic in it always ; I must be kept well out of sight. They like the bull or the swan well enough : but once let them set eyes on *me*, and they are frightened out of their lives.

Eros. Well, of course. They are but mortals ; the sight of Zeus is too much for them.

Zeus. Then why are Branchus and Hyacinth so fond of Apollo ?

64 *Dialogues of the Gods, ij*

Eros. Daphne ran away from him, anyhow; in spite of his beautiful hair and his smooth chin. Now, shall I tell you the way to win hearts? Keep that aegis of yours quiet, and leave the thunderbolt at home; make yourself as smart as you can; curl your hair and tie it up with a bit of ribbon, get a purple cloak, and gold-bespangled shoes, and march forth to the music of flute and drum;—and see if you don't get a finer following than Dionysus, for all his Maenads.

Zeus. Pooh! I'll win no hearts on such terms.

Eros. Oh, in that case, don't fall in love. Nothing could be simpler.

Zeus. I dare say; but I *like* being in love, only I don't like all this fuss. Now mind; if I let you off, it is on this understanding.   F.

III

Zeus. Hermes

Zeus. Hermes, you know Inachus's beautiful daughter?

Her. I do. Io, you mean?

Zeus. Yes; she is not a girl now, but a heifer.

Her. Magic at work! how did that come about?

Zeus. Hera had a jealous fit, and transformed her. But that is not all; she has thought of a new punishment for the poor thing. She has put a cowherd in charge, who is all over eyes; this Argus, as he is called, pastures the heifer, and never goes to sleep.

Her. Well, what am I to do?

Zeus. Fly down to Nemea, where the pasture is, kill Argus, take Io across the sea to Egypt, and convert her into Isis. She shall be henceforth an Egyptian Goddess, flood the Nile, regulate the winds, and rescue mariners.   H.

APPENDIX (ii)
Historical Ordering of *Dialogues of the Gods*

As noted in Appendix (i), until William Tooke's translation of 1820, Lucian's editors up to that point had played fairly fast and loose with the ordering of the *Dialogues of the Gods*, often disregarding the "traditional" ordering of the source documents.

In John Carr's *Dialogues of Lucian* (1773), only eight of the twenty-six *Dialogues of the Gods* are included, leaving eighteen excised. These eight are re-ordered.

In Thomas Francklin's *The Works of Lucian* (1780) the dialogues are again re-ordered, and seemingly as the mood took him, so that we flit between Hades, the River Styx, Olympus, and the high seas. All of the *Dialogues of the Gods* are however included.

William Tooke's *Lucian of Samosata* (1820) and Howard Williams' *Lucian's Dialogues* (1888) are selected works, but *Dialogues of the Gods* is complete in both, and both follow the traditional ordering exactly.

In Henry and Frank Fowler's *The Works of Lucian of Samosata* (1905) the traditional ordering is again followed exactly, although seven are excised.

This edition re-orders *Dialogues of the Gods* in a bid for narrative consistency, but is complete. *The Judgement of Paris* is included in Appendix (iii).

The table overleaf delineates all these decisions dialogue-by-dialogue. At the very least this may help clear up some of the confusion I encountered when first assembling this edition, and prove useful to editors of the future.

Historical Ordering of *Dialogues of the Gods*	SOURCES IN GREEK	CARR 1774	FRANCKLIN 1780	TOOKE 1820	WILLIAMS 1888	FOWLER 1905	THIS ED. 2016
Prometheus & Zeus	1	3	14	1	1	1	2
Eros & Zeus	2	4	15	2	2	2	3
Zeus & Hermes	3	—	1	3	3	3	9
Zeus & Ganymede	4	—	16	4	4	—	6
Hera & Zeus	5	—	18	5	5	—	7
Hera & Zeus	6	—	19	6	6	6	8
Hephaestus & Apollo	7	5	2	7	7	7	4
Hephaestus & Zeus	8	6	3	8	8	8	1
Poseidon & Hermes	9	7	17	9	9	—	5
Hermes & Helios	10	—	20	10	10	—	10
Aphrodite & Selene	11	—	21	11	11	11	11
Aphrodite & Eros	12	—	4	12	12	12	12
Zeus, Asclepius & Heracles	13	2	5	13	13	13	19
Hermes & Apollo	14	—	6	14	14	14	13
Hermes & Apollo	15	—	22	15	15	15	14
Hera & Leto	16	—	7	16	16	16	15
Apollo & Hermes	17	—	23	17	17	—	16
Hera & Zeus	18	—	8	18	18	18	17
Aphrodite & Eros	19	—	9	19	19	19	18
The Judgement of Paris	20	—	26	20	20	20	A
Ares & Hermes	21	1	10	21	21	21	20
Pan & Hermes	22	—	24	22	22	—	21
Apollo & Dionysus	23	—	25	23	23	—	22
Hermes & Maia	24	—	11	24	24	24	23
Zeus & Helios	25	8	12	25	25	25	24
Apollo & Hermes	26	—	13	26	26	26	25
	'Trad.'	*Partial conflated*	*Partial conflated*	*'Trad.'*	*'Trad.'*	*'Trad.; expurgated*	*For narrative consistency*

APPENDIX (iii)
The Judgement of Paris

Readers already familiar with Lucian and particularly *Dialogues of the Gods* may have noticed that the *The Judgement of Paris* is not included in the main text of this new edition. While all previous translations of *Dialogues of the Gods* include within them *The Judgement of Paris*, I have, for practical reasons, made the decision to instead place it here in the appendices.

The Judgement involves a crowd of six speakers instead of the more usual two, and is a much longer read. In this sense it is something of an anomaly anyway, and, it seems to me, sits itself rather separately from the other dialogues. (Indeed, some modern scholars do separate it from the other, numbered dialogues by assigning to it a letter, "A", rather than listing it as the 26th dialogue.) But critically, had I applied to this dialogue the same typographic system that forms the basis of this book's design, it would have collapsed that system and what I felt would make for a novel and enjoyable reading experience.

I hope readers will agree with this decision, and look generously upon any suspicions of sophistry. The version that follows is from the Fowler edition, translated by Frank.

The Judgement of Paris:
Zeus, Aphrodite, Hera, Hermes, Athena & Paris

Zeus. Hermes, take this apple, and go with it to Phrygia; on the Gargaran peak of Ida you will find Priam's son, the herdsman. Give him this message: "Paris, because you are handsome, and wise in the things of love, Zeus commands you to judge between the Goddesses, and say which is the most beautiful. And the prize shall be this apple." Now, you three, there is no time to be lost: away with you to your judge. I will have nothing to do with the matter: I love you all exactly alike, and I only wish you could all three win. If I were to give the prize to one of you, the other two would hate me, of course. In these circumstances, I am ill qualified to be your judge. But this young Phrygian to whom you are going is of the royal blood—a relation of Ganymede's—and at the same time a simple countryman; so that we need have no hesitation in trusting his eyes.

Aphrodite. As far as I am concerned, Zeus, Momus himself might be our judge; I should not be afraid to show myself. What fault could he find with me? But the others must agree too.

Hera. Oh, we are under no alarm, thank you—though your admirer Ares should be appointed. But Paris will do; whoever Paris is.

Zeus. And my little Athena; have we her approval? Nay, never blush, nor hide your face. Well, well, maidens will be coy; 'tis a delicate subject. But there, she nods consent. Now, off with you; and mind, the beaten ones must not be cross with the judge; I will not have the poor lad harmed. The prize of beauty can be but one.

Hermes. Now for Phrygia. I will show the way; keep close behind me, ladies, and don't be nervous. I know Paris well: he is a charming young man; a great gallant, and an admirable judge of beauty. Depend on it, he will make a good award.

Aphrodite. I am glad to hear that; I ask for nothing better than a just judge. Has he a wife, Hermes, or is he a bachelor?

Hermes. Not exactly a bachelor.

Aphrodite. What do you mean?

Hermes. I believe there is a wife, as it were; a good enough sort of girl—a native of those parts—but sadly countrified! I fancy he does not care very much about her. Why do you ask?

Aphrodite. I just wanted to know.

Athena. Now, Hermes, that is not fair. No whispering with Aphrodite.

Hermes. It was nothing, Athena; nothing about you. She only asked me whether Paris was a bachelor.

Athena. What business is that of hers?

Hermes. None that I know of. She meant nothing by the question; she just wanted to know.

Athena. Well, and is he?

Hermes. Why, no.

Athena. And does he care for military glory? Has he ambition? Or is he a mere neatherd?

Hermes. I couldn't say for certain. But he is a young man, so it is to be presumed that distinction on the field of battle is among his desires.

Aphrodite. There, you see; I don't complain; I say nothing when you whisper with her. Aphrodite is not so particular as some people.

Hermes. Athena asked me almost exactly the same as you did; so don't be cross. It will do you no harm, my answering a plain question. Meanwhile, we have left the stars far behind us, and are almost over Phrygia. There is Ida: I can make out the peak of Gargarum quite plainly; and if I am not mistaken, there is Paris himself.

Hera. Where is he? I don't see him.

Hermes. Look over there to the left, Hera: not on the top, but down the side, by that cave where you see the herd.

Hera. But I don't see the herd.

Hermes. What, don't you see them coming out from between the rocks— where I am pointing, look—and the man running down from the crag, and keeping them together with his staff?

Hera. I see him now; if he it is.

Hermes. Oh, that is Paris. But we are getting near; it is time to alight and walk. He might be frightened, if we were to descend upon him so suddenly.

Hera. Yes; very well. And now that we are on the earth, you might go on ahead, Aphrodite, and show us the way. You know the country, of course, having been here so often to see Anchises; or so I have heard.

Aphrodite. Your sneers are thrown away on me, Hera.

Hermes. Come; I'll lead the way myself. I spent some time on Ida, while Zeus was courting Ganymede. Many is the time that I have been sent here to keep watch over the boy; and when at last the eagle came, I flew by his side, and helped him with his lovely burden. This is the very rock, if I remember; yes, Ganymede was piping to his sheep, when down swooped the eagle behind him, and tenderly, oh, so tenderly, caught him up in those talons, and with the turban in his beak bore him off, the frightened boy straining his neck the while to see his captor. I picked up his pipes—he had dropped them in his fright and—ah! Here is our umpire, close at hand. Let us accost him. Good-morrow, herdsman!

Paris. Good-morrow, youngster. And who may you be, who come thus far afield? And these dames? They are over comely, to be wandering on the mountain-side.

Hermes. These "dames", good Paris, are Hera, Athena, and Aphrodite; and I am Hermes, with a message from Zeus. Why so pale and tremulous? Compose yourself; there is nothing the matter. Zeus appoints you the judge of their beauty. "Because you are handsome, and wise in the things of love" (so runs the message), "I leave the decision to you; and for the prize—read the inscription on the apple."

Paris. Let me see what it is about. FOR THE FAIR, it says. But, my lord Hermes, how shall a mortal and a rustic like myself be judge of such unparalleled beauty? This is no sight for a herdsman's eyes; let the fine city folk decide on such matters. As for me, I can tell you which of two goats is the fairer beast; or I can judge betwixt heifer and heifer—'tis my trade. But here, where all are beautiful alike, I know not how a man may leave looking at one, to look upon another. Where my eyes fall, there they fasten—for there is beauty: I move them, and what do I find? More loveliness! I am fixed again, yet distracted by neighbouring charms. I bathe in beauty. I am enthralled: ah, why am I not all eyes like Argus? Methinks it were a fair award, to give the apple to all three.

Then again: one is the wife and sister of Zeus; the others are his daughters. Take it where you will, 'tis a hard matter to judge.

Hermes. So it is, Paris. At the same time—Zeus' orders! There is no way out of it.

Paris. Well, please point out to them, Hermes, that the losers must not be angry with me; the fault will be in my eyes only.

Hermes. That is quite understood. And now to work.

Paris. I must do what I can; there is no help for it. But first let me ask—am I just to look at them as they are, or must I go into the matter thoroughly?

Hermes. That is for you to decide, in virtue of your office. You have only to give your orders; it is as you think best.

Paris. As I think best? Then I will be thorough.

Hermes. Get ready, ladies. Now, Mr. Umpire—I will look the other way.

Hera. I approve your decision, Paris. I will be the first to submit myself to your inspection. You shall see that I have more to boast of than white arms and large eyes: nought of me but is beautiful.

Paris. Aphrodite, will you also prepare?

Athena. Oh, Paris—make her take off that girdle, first; there is magic in it; she will bewitch you. For that matter, she has no right to come thus tricked out and painted—just like a courtesan! She ought to show herself unadorned.

Paris. They are right about the girdle, madam; it must go.

Aphrodite. Oh, very well, Athena: then take off that helmet, and show your head bare, instead of trying to intimidate the judge with that waving plume. I suppose you are afraid the colour of your eyes may be noticed, without their formidable surroundings.

Athena. Oh, here is my helmet.

Aphrodite. And here is my girdle.

Hera. Now then.

Paris. God of wonders! What loveliness is here! Oh, rapture! How exquisite these maiden charms! How dazzling the majesty of Heaven's true queen! And oh, how sweet, how enthralling is Aphrodite's smile! 'Tis too much, too much of happiness. But perhaps it would be well for me to view each in detail; for as yet I doubt, and know not where to look; my eyes are drawn all ways at once.

Aphrodite. Yes, that will be best.

Paris. Withdraw then, you and Athena; and let Hera remain.

Hera. So be it; and when you have finished your scrutiny, you have next to consider, how you would like the present which I offer you. Paris, give me the prize of beauty, and you shall be lord of all Asia.

Paris. I will take no presents. Withdraw. I shall judge as I think right. Approach, Athena.

Athena. Behold. And, Paris, if you will say that I am the fairest, I will make you a great warrior and conqueror, and you shall always win, in every one of your battles.

Paris. But I have nothing to do with fighting, Athena. As you see, there is peace throughout all Lydia and Phrygia, and my father's dominion is uncontested. But never mind; I am not going to take your present, but you shall have fair play. You can robe again and put on your helmet; I have seen. And now for Aphrodite.

Aphrodite. Here I am; take your time, and examine carefully; let nothing escape your vigilance. And I have something else to say to you, handsome Paris. Yes, you handsome boy, I have long had an eye on you; I think you must be the handsomest young fellow in all Phrygia. But it is such a pity that you don't leave these rocks and crags, and live in a town; you will lose all your beauty in this desert. What have you to do with mountains? What satisfaction can your beauty give to a lot of cows? You ought to have been married long ago; not to any of these dowdy women hereabouts, but to some Greek girl; an Argive, perhaps, or a Corinthian, or a Spartan; Helen, now, is a Spartan, and such a pretty girl—quite as pretty as I am—and so susceptible! Why, if she once caught sight of you, she would give up everything, I am sure, to go with you, and a most devoted wife she would be. But you have heard of Helen, of course?

Paris. No, ma'am; but I should like to hear all about her now.

Aphrodite. Well, she is the daughter of Leda, the beautiful woman, you know, whom Zeus visited in the disguise of a swan.

Paris. And what is she like?

Aphrodite. She is fair, as might be expected from the swan, soft as down (she was hatched from an egg, you know), and such a lithe, graceful figure; and only think, she is so much admired, that there was a war because Theseus ran away with her; and she was a mere child then. And when she grew up, the very first men in Greece were suitors for her hand, and she was given to Menelaus, who is descended from Pelops. Now, if you like, she shall be your wife.

Paris. What, when she is married already?

Aphrodite. Tut, child, you are a simpleton: I understand these things.

Paris. I should like to understand them too.

Aphrodite. You will set out for Greece on a tour of inspection: and when you get to Sparta, Helen will see you; and for the rest—her falling in love, and going back with you—that will be my affair.

Paris. But that is what I cannot believe—that she will forsake her husband to cross the seas with a stranger, a barbarian.

Aphrodite. Trust me for that. I have two beautiful children, Love and Desire. They shall be your guides. Love will assail her in all his might, and compel her to love you: Desire will encompass you about, and make you desirable and lovely as himself; and I will be there to help. I can get the Graces to come too, and between us we shall prevail.

Paris. How this will end, I know not. All I do know is, that I am in love with Helen already. I see her before me—I sail for Greece—I am in Sparta—I am on my homeward journey, with her at my side! Ah, why is none of it true?

Aphrodite. Wait. Do not fall in love yet. You have first to secure my interest with the bride, by your award. The union must be graced with my victorious presence: your marriage-feast shall be my feast of victory. Love, beauty, wedlock; all these you may purchase at the price of yonder apple.

Paris. But perhaps after the award you will forget all about me?

Aphrodite. Shall I swear?

Paris. No; but promise once more.

Aphrodite. I promise that you shall have Helen to wife; that she shall follow you, and make Troy her home; and I will be present with you, and help you in all.

Paris. And bring Love, and Desire, and the Graces?

Aphrodite. Assuredly; and Passion and Hymen as well.

Paris. Take the apple: it is yours.

Lucian's Dream

From this short and entertaining autobiographical essay we glean almost everything we know about Lucian as a man, and so I felt it would be both helpful and revealing to reproduce it in full here. The text is from the Fowler edition, translated by Henry.

Lucian's Dream

When my childhood was over, and I had just left school, my father called a council to decide upon my profession. Most of his friends considered that the life of culture was very exacting in toil, time, and money: a life only for fortune's favourites; whereas our resources were quite narrow, and urgently called for relief. If I were to take up some ordinary handicraft, I should be making my own living straight off, instead of eating my father's meat at my age; and before long my earnings would be a welcome contribution.

So the next step was to select the most satisfactory of the handicrafts; it must be one quite easy to acquire, respectable, inexpensive as regards plant, and fairly profitable. Various suggestions were made, according to the taste and knowledge of the councillors; but my father turned to my mother's brother, supposed to be an excellent statuary, and said to him: "With you here, it would be a sin to prefer any other craft; take the lad, regard him as your charge, teach him to handle, match, and grave your marble; he will do well enough; you know he has the ability." This he had inferred from certain tricks I used to play with wax. When I got out of school, I used to scrape off the wax from my tablets and work it into cows, horses, or even men and women, and he thought I did it creditably; my masters used to cane me for it, but on this occasion it was taken as evidence of a natural faculty, and my modelling gave them good hopes of my picking up the art quickly.

As soon as it seemed convenient for me to begin, I was handed over to my uncle, and by no means reluctantly; I thought I should find it amusing, and be in a position to impress my companions; they should see me chiselling gods and making little images for myself and my favourites. The usual first experience of beginners followed: my uncle gave me a chisel, and told me to give a gentle touch to a plaque lying on the bench: "Well begun is half done," said he, not very originally. In my inexperience I brought down the tool too hard, and the plaque broke; he flew into a rage, picked up a stick which lay handy, and gave me an introduction to art which might have been gentler and more encouraging; so I paid my footing with tears.

I ran off, and reached home still howling and tearful, told the story of the stick, and showed my bruises. I said a great deal about his brutality, and added that it was all envy: he was afraid of my being a better sculptor than he. My mother was very angry, and abused her brother roundly; as for me, I fell asleep that night with my eyes still wet, and sorrow was with me till the morning.

So much of my tale is ridiculous and childish. What you have now to hear is not so contemptible, but deserves an attentive hearing; in the words of Homer,

> To me in slumber wrapt a dream divine
> Ambrosial night conveyed,

a dream so vivid as to be indistinguishable from reality; after all these years, I have still the figures of its persons in my eyes, the vibration of their words in my ears; so clear it all was.

Two women had hold of my hands, and were trying vehemently and persistently to draw me each her way; I was nearly pulled in two with their contention; now one would prevail and all but get entire possession of me, now I would fall to the other again, All the time they were exchanging loud protests: "He is mine, and I mean to keep him;" "Not yours at all, and it is no use your saying he is." One of them seemed to be a working woman, masculine looking, with untidy hair, horny hands, and dress kilted up; she was all powdered with plaster, like my uncle when he was chipping marble. The other had a beautiful face, a comely figure, and neat attire. At last they invited me to decide which of them I would live with; the rough manly one made her speech first.

"Dear youth, I am Statuary—the art which you yesterday began to learn, and which has a natural and a family claim upon you. Your grandfather" (naming my mother's father) "and both your uncles practised it, and it brought them credit. If you will turn a deaf ear to this person's foolish cajolery, and come and live with me, I promise you wholesome food and good strong muscles; you shall never fear envy, never leave your country and your people to go wandering abroad, and you shall be commended not for your words, but for your works.

"Let not a slovenly person or dirty clothes repel you; such were the conditions of that Phidias who produced the Zeus, of Polyclitus who created the Hera, of the much-lauded Myron, of the admired Praxiteles; and all these are worshipped with the Gods. If you should come to be counted among them, you will surely have fame enough for yourself through all the world, you will make your father the envy of all fathers, and bring your country to all men's notice." This and more said Statuary, stumbling along in a strange jargon, stringing her arguments together in a very earnest manner, and quite intent on persuading me. But I can remember no more; the greater part of it has faded from my memory. When she stopped, the other's turn came.

"And I, child, am Culture, no stranger to you even now, though you have yet to make my closer acquaintance. The advantages that the profession of a sculptor will bring with it you have just been told; they amount to no more than being a worker with your hands, your whole prospects in life limited to that; you will be obscure, poorly and illiberally paid, mean-spirited, of no account outside your doors; your influence will never help a friend, silence an enemy, nor impress your countrymen; you will be just a worker, one of the masses, cowering before the distinguished, truckling to the eloquent, living the life of a hare, a prey to your betters. You may turn out a Phidias or a Polyclitus, to be sure, and create a number of wonderful works; but even so, though your art will be generally commended, no sensible observer will be found to wish himself like you; whatever your real qualities, you will always rank as a common craftsman who makes his living with his hands.

"Be governed by me, on the other hand, and your first reward shall be a view of the many wondrous deeds and doings of the men of old; you shall hear their words and know them all, what manner of men they were; and your soul, which is your very self, I will adorn with many fair adornments, with self-mastery and justice and reverence and mildness, with consideration and understanding and fortitude, with love of what is beautiful, and yearning for what is great; these things it is that are the true and pure ornaments of the soul. Naught shall escape you either of ancient wisdom or of present avail; nay, the future too, with me to aid, you shall foresee; in a word, I will instill into you, and that in no long time, all knowledge human and divine.

"This penniless son of who knows whom, contemplating but now a vocation so ignoble, shall soon be admired and envied of all, with honour and praise and the fame of high achievement, respected by the high-born and the affluent, clothed as I am clothed" (and here she pointed to her own bright raiment), "held worthy of place and precedence; and if you leave your native land, you will be no unknown nameless wanderer; you shall wear my marks upon you, and every man beholding you shall touch his neighbour's arm and say, That is he.

"And if some great moment come to try your friends or country, then shall all look to you. And to your lightest word the many shall listen open-mouthed, and marvel, and count you happy in your eloquence, and your father in his son. 'Tis said that some from mortal men become immortal; and I will make it truth in you; for though you depart from life yourself, you shall keep touch with the learned and hold communion with the best. Consider the mighty Demosthenes, whose son he was, and whither I exalted him; consider Aeschines; how came a Philip to pay court to the cymbal-woman's brat? How but for my sake? Dame Statuary here had the breeding of Socrates himself; but no sooner could he discern the better part, than he deserted her and enlisted with me; since when, his name is on every tongue.

"You may dismiss all these great men, and with them all glorious deeds, majestic words, and seemly looks, all honour, repute, praise, precedence, power, and office, all lauded eloquence and envied wisdom; these you may put from you, to gird on a filthy apron and assume a servile guise; then will you handle crowbars and graving tools, mallets and chisels; you will be bowed over your work, with eyes and thoughts bent earthwards, abject as abject can be, with never a free and manly upward look or aspiration; all your care will be to proportion and fairly drape your works; to proportioning and adorning yourself you will give little heed enough, making yourself of less account than your marble."

I waited not for her to bring her words to an end, but rose up and spoke my mind; I turned from that clumsy mechanic woman, and went rejoicing to lady Culture, the more when I thought upon the stick, and all the blows my yesterday's apprenticeship had brought me. For a time the deserted one was wroth, with clenched fists and grinding teeth; but at last she stiffened, like another

Niobe, into marble. A strange fate, but I must request your belief; dreams are great magicians, are they not?

Then the other looked upon me and spoke: "For this justice done me," said she, "you shall now be recompensed; come, mount this car"—and lo, one stood ready, drawn by winged steeds like Pegasus—"that you may learn what fair sights another choice would have cost you." We mounted, she took the reins and drove, and I was carried aloft and beheld towns and nations and peoples from the East to the West; and methought I was sowing like Triptolemus; but the nature of the seed I cannot call to mind—only this, that men on earth when they saw it gave praise, and all whom I reached in my flight sent me on my way with blessings.

When she had presented these things to my eyes, and me to my admirers, she brought me back, no more clad as when my flight began; I returned, methought, in glorious raiment. And finding my father where he stood waiting, she showed him my raiment, and the guise in which I came, and said a word to him upon the lot which they had come so near appointing for me. All this I saw when scarce out of my childhood; the confusion and terror of the stick, it may be, stamped it on my memory.

"Good gracious," says someone, before I have done, "what a long-winded lawyer's vision!" "This," interrupts another, "must be a winter dream, to judge by the length of night required; or perhaps it took three nights, like the making of Heracles. What has come over him, that he babbles such puerilities? Memorable things indeed, a child in bed, and a very ancient, worn-out dream! What stale frigid stuff! Does he take us for interpreters of dreams?" I do not. When Xenophon related that vision of his which you all know, of his father's house on fire and the rest, was it just by way of a riddle? Was it in deliberate ineptitude that he reproduced it? A likely thing in their desperate military situation, with the enemy surrounding them! No, the relation was to serve a useful purpose.

Similarly I have had an object in telling you my dream. It is that the young may be guided to the better way and set themselves to Culture, especially any among them who is recreant for fear of poverty, and minded to enter the wrong path, to the ruin of a nature not all ignoble. Such a one will be strengthened by my tale, I am well assured; in me he will find an apt example; let him only compare the boy of those days, who started in pursuit of the best and devoted himself to Culture regardless of immediate poverty, with the man who has now come back to you, as high in fame, to put it at the lowest, as any stonecutter of them all.

AFTERWORD

Lucian's razor-sharp and amusing satires, aimed at the authority figures of his day, worked. No one whose reputation he speared fully recovered from the assault, regardless of whether they were philosophers, priests, kings, or gods.

Lucian is useful to us because he is always searching for the sore point in his readers as well as his subjects. Testing as often as he clarifies, he perceived, and helps us to perceive, that moral authorities are typically—necessarily— humourless. This is true particularly when it comes to the subject of themselves, whatever age or culture they live in; and therefore, that humour must become the key constituent of a counteracting humanism, the weapon of first and last resort in the battle against intellectual, spiritual, or moral self-righteousness.

Reading his dialogues today, we might begin to wonder what he would have made of our current crop of authority figures. In a world still largely at heel to the gross whims and hypocrisies of tyranny, ideology, and celebrity— a collection of bad ideas often knitted together into one terrible, high-definition bundle—Lucian's ideas still resonate. They might resonate most of all in Syria, the region of Lucian's birth, where the appreciation of humanism and human- ity—humour—seems to have reached an all-time low.

We might be grateful that enough admirers have dedicatedly researched, compiled, and translated Lucian's work to ensure that it is at least recorded in something close to its entirety. We might also be grateful that much of it is now available for anyone to enjoy for free on the web, though Lucian is rather lost there except to those who might deliberately set out to follow the strands that lead to him. Perhaps this book can go a small way towards inspiring that journey; I hope so.

Nicholas Jeeves
Cambridge, March 2016

ACKNOWLEDGEMENTS

Work on this project was made all the more pleasurable thanks to the assistance of several people, each of whom deserves special mention here.

Firstly, thanks to Adam Green, editor of *The Public Domain Review* and my publisher at PDR Press, for his continued support and enthusiasm for this book. *The Public Domain Review* remains a great source of entertainment, information, and inspiration. I heartily recommend a visit: www.publicdomainreview. org. If you do and find you have enjoyed yourself, please consider becoming a valued "Friend of *The Public Domain Review*".

Grateful thanks must also go to Frank Redmond, the man behind the *The Lucian of Samosata Project*, an online resource collating numerous translations, quotations, biographical details, commentaries, references and links devoted to Lucian. Frank personally assisted me with a number of tricky questions, particularly pertaining to the ordering of the dialogues. I hope the re-ordering that I have imposed on them here meets with his approval. You can find *The Lucian of Samosata Project* at www.lucianofsamosata.info.

Finally I would like to record notes of thanks to Will Hill, my friend and colleague at Cambridge School of Art, who listened to my frequent rhapsodising about Lucian with characteristic patience and benign expectation; and to Sten King, who supported the project from the first and provided necessary encouragement.

Aside from the key translations of Lucian's works, all of which are available online, Jenny McMorris' excellent biography of Henry Fowler, *The Warden of English* (OUP, 2001) proved invaluable when learning about his life preceding the publication of *The Works of Lucian of Samosata*. Henry's life and adventures became more interesting still after 1905 and McMorris' book expertly chronicles them.

With thanks to The Friends of The Public Domain Review *for their ongoing support:*

A. P. Guttshall, Adele Fasick, Adrienne Anderson, Aemilia Scott, Afton Lorraine Woodward, Albert Jaccoma, Alé Mercado, Alembic Rare Books, Alexander Nirenberg, Alison Bell, Alissa Likavec, Allana Mayer, Allegra, A. M. Emerson, Amanda Glassman, Amity Michelina, Amy Harmon, Ana Méndez de Andés, Andrea Callow, Andrea Vela Alarcon, Andres Saenz De Sicilia, Andrew Chapman, Andrew Clifford Pinder, Andrew O'Kelly, Andrew Seeder, Anne Marie Houppert, Annie Johns, Antonio Merenda, Anzan Hoshin, Armitage Shanks, ARTEL, Artist's Proof Editions, avianovum, Barbara Ruef, Bea Hartman, Bella Terra Publishing, Ben Bradley, Bertrand Monier, Betsy Pohlman, Braden Pemberton, Bree Burns, Brian Floca, Brian Harmon, Bryan Gardiner, Burton Cromer, Buster T. Kallikak Jr, Caitlin Keegan, Cally Wight, Candia McWilliam, Carl Taylor, Caroline Carlson, Cathy Sandifer, Cei Lambert, Cheryl Powell, Chris Burns, Christian Fredrik Aronsen, Christian Jones, Christina Hammermeister, Christine A. Jones, Christine Kanownik, Christopher Hughes, Cigornia, Cindy Womack, Clara Bosak-Schroeder, Claudio Ruiz, clickscape.net, Colin Fanning, Corey Chimko, Cowbelles, Cristina Bryan, Curtis Thomas, D. P. Carroll, Dan MacDuff, Danae Panchaud, Daniel F., Daniel Lander, Daniela Didier, Darcie DeAngelo, David Bryan, David Chatwin, David Conolly, David Palmeter, David Sharpe, David Wolske, Debi Geroux, Deborah Weber, Deborah Woodman, Diane Fox, Diane Mayr, Dictionary of Sydney, Dina Eastwood, Dipesh Navsaria, Donna Emsel Schill, Doug Harris, Dr Natalie McDonagh, Dr David Abbey, Dr Lauren K. Robinson, Dr Omed, Dr Steven R. Miller, Dry Toasts, Dylan Flesch, E. Lee Eltzroth, E. A. Craig, Edinburgh Medical School, Elettra Gorni, Elizabeth Novak, Elizabeth Rowe, Elizabeth Van Pelt, Elly Catelli, Elvira Piedra, Emily Forgot, Emily H. Cohen, Erica H. Smith, Erik Spiekermann, Erin Fletcher Singley, Erin McKean, Eugenia Leftwich, Far Beyond Film LLC, Fiona Winifred Wood, Foxpath IND, Frank Kloos, Frank Modica, Futureofthebook, Gail Horvath, Giampaolo Luparia, Gloria Katz Huyck, Greg Lehman, Grow House Grow, Guglielmo Centini, Hannah Jenkins, Hannah Margolin, Harald Walter Azmann, Heather Hogan, Heavy Eyes, Henrietta Rose-Innes, Hilde Luytens, Ian Herbert, Ideum, infoclio.ch Swiss portal for the historical sciences, Jack O'Connor, Jackie Brooks, Jackie May, Jake DeBacher, Jakia, James Ashner, James Cox, James Downs, James West, Janie Geiser, Jaye Bartell, Jeanne Marie Neumann, Jed Lackritz, Jeff Diver, Jeffrey Brian Hanington, Jeffrey Turco, Jemima McDonald, Jennifer A. Meagher, Jenny Burger & Jordan Carroll, Jenny Molloy, Jenny Zigzag, Jesse L., Jesse U., Jesseca Ferguson, Jessie Huffaker, J. F. & Penelope Englert, Jill Littlewood, Jim Erickson, Joanne Koreman, jockjimy, Jodie Robson, Joe Virbasius, John Aboud, John Barrett, John Cooper, John Doba, John J. Griffiths, John Lopez, John Phillip Cooper, John R. Gibson, John Rooke, John Son, Jonathan Geer, Jonathan Gray, Jonathan Green, Jonathan Hirshon, Jonathan Lamb, Jordan Guzzardo, Jose M. Diaz, Joseph McAlhany, Judith Field, Judy Hill, Julie Green, Julie Heller, Julie Trainor, K. Shafer, Karen Bonsignore, Kate Borowske, Katharine Pitt, Katherine Alexander, Katherine Hall, Kathleen Sweeney, Kati Schardl, Katy Cherry, Katy Liljeholm, Keith Calder, Kerrie & Simon Triggs, Keven Eyre, Kristen Gallerneaux, Kristie Mitchell,

Kristine M. Richards, Lahela Nihipali, L. D. Gunther, L. E. Usher, Lang Thompson, Larry A. Schroeder, Laura Gibbs, Laura Griffiths, Laura Lorson, Laura Macfehin, Laura Stein, Lauren Turner, Lawrence Wilkinson, LCTV, Leslie Gardner, Lieke Ploeger, Lightner Museum, Lilith Saintcrow, Lillian Wilkie, Lincoln County Television, Linda Bourke, Lindsay Van Niekerk, Lisa G. O'Sullivan, Liz Folk, Liza Daly, Lizzie Seal, L. M. Rima, Lois Blood Bennett, Lucia Mesak, Lujean Martin, Luke Sperduto, Luna Labrabeagle, Lydia Pyne, Lynn Rogan, Lynne Pate, Maggie Simonelli, Magpie Bookshop, Malibu Carl, Marcia Moore, Marcus Ivarsson, Margaret E. Smith, Margery Meadow, Margherita Peliti, Maria Castello, Marina Montanaro, Marina Nichols, Marjory Lehan, Mark Cohen, Mark David Kaufman, Mark H. Larick, Mark Stein, Marly Gisser, Martha J. Fleischman, Martin L. Smith, Martin S. Lindsay, Mary Fletcher, Mary Margaret Cronin, Matt Mullin, Matthew J. Smith, Maureen Forys, Meaghan Walsh Gerard, Meg Rosenburg, Megan Orpwood-Russell, Meghanne Phillips, Melinda McDonald, Melisande Charles, Meredith Sward, Michael Lang, Michael Martone, Michael Mejia, Michael W. Young, Mo, Moran Shoub, Muffie Meyer, Nancy C. Tipton, Nathan Fowler, Nathan Maxwell Cann, Nathaniel Tarn, Nicholas de Godoy Lopes, Nigel Algar, Nikolaj Sømod, Nolan Bennett, Noumena Press, Occulto Magazine, Oficina de Arquitectura, Olga Zilberbourg, Orly Yadin & Bob Summers, Oscar Byrne, Outsiderart, Pardo Fornaciari, Parker Higgins, Patrick R. Cleary, Pattern Research Inc., Patti Gibbons, Paul Harrington, Paula Russell Weiss, Penelope Swan, Peter Brown, Peter Fleck, Peter Fontilus, Philippe Vilon, Phox Pop Magazine, Pia, Pil Lindgreen K., Pim Bendt, pole/go, Prof. Shorthair, Prof. José Enrique Pons MD, Prue Dixon, Queer Astrology Project, Rachel Robbins, Ramiro Pascual, Rayn, Rebecca Clark, Rebecca Resinski, Rechtsanwalt Christian Kramarz LL.M., René Anderson Benitz, Retrogrouch, Richard Stim, Rob E., Robert Ashton Jarman, Robert Vowles, Roberto Tejada, Rob P. Stern, Robyn Hugo McIntyre, Ron Sims, Rufus Pollock, Ruthie Dornfeld, Sacramennah, Sander Feinberg, Sandra Huston, Sara Mörtsell, Sarah Barton, Sarah E. Gentile, Sarah Louise Bishop, Sarah Zar, Sashareen Morgan, Scout Paget, Self-Publishing Review, Seth Lederer, Shannon Walsh, Sharon, Shyan Y., Sigmund Petersen, Silvia Fernandez, Silvia Sanchez Di Martino, Simone L. Havel, Sonya L. Moore, Stephanie Pierson, Stephen Bohrer, Stephen Stinehour, Stephen Thomas, Steve Booth, Steve Hynds, Stuart Chittenden, Susan Kern, Susan Post, Susan Prior, Susan Serna, Susie B., Suzanne Fox, Suzanne Frances Smith, Suzanne Simon, Suzy Byrnes, Sylvia Wu, Tad Kline, Tanja M. Cupples Meece, Terrence McDermott, Terri Parsons, Terry Harpold, Tessa Hunkin, Thinkfarm Interactive Inc., Thomas E. Thunders, Thomas F. Dillingham, TIME/IMAGE, Tin Fischer, Tina Sakura, Tod Mesirow, Robot Body Inc., Tom Fenyll, Tracey Genet, Valentin Bakardjiev, Vibhu Mittal, Vicky Loebel, Vince O'Connor, Walter Schoenknecht, Wanderlust Ceramics, Wellcome Library, Whitworth and I, William B. Holden, William B. Ashworth Jr, Wilton Gorske, Wolfgang Schlüter, Y. D. Bar-Ness, Yoonmi Nam, Zachary Barnhart, Zarino Zappia, Zuzka Kurtz.

Learn more about The Friends of The Public Domain Review *and how you can help support the project here: publicdomainreview.org/support.*

Lightning Source UK Ltd.
Milton Keynes UK
UKOW07f0845111216

289672UK00010B/26/P